ALL IN

A Collection of Essays on Christian
Living
The Greatest Commandment
Bearing Fruit
A Sabbath Rest
Holiness
Eternal Impact

By Daniel Bartlett

Daniel Bartlett

All In

First published in the United States by Daniel Bartlett

ISBN: 979-8-9898013-0-5

Library of Congress Control Number: 2024900273

Contact: Threshingstone@gmail.com

Daniel Bartlett

All In

TABLE OF CONTENTS

Daniel Bartlett

Introduction

"And you shall remember the whole way that the LORD your God has led you these forty years in the wilderness, that he might humble you, testing you to know what was in your heart, whether you would keep his commandments or not." - Deuteronomy 8:2[1]

My deep desire over the years has been to walk closely with Jesus, to know him, honor him, and be used by him. But I have had a lot of questions of how I am supposed to do that well in our world of constant distractions, endless entertainment, and cultural noise. As I've walked with the Lord, I believe that he has taught me things through his Word about walking with him, and these are the things that I'd like to share with you.

In my life, I have found that I am very prone to forget, to forget what the Lord has done in my life and to forget and stray from what he has taught me. It was because of this that two years ago I began my quest to remember. I began writing down what the Lord has taught me over the years of walking with him. This book is the product of that endeavor. I never intended these lessons to become a book, but as I've written and then gone back over the years to read what I wrote down, I've been blessed over and over again by remembering. And I want to share that blessing with you.

In the following pages, I've recorded some of what I consider to be the foundational teachings of the Lord in my life. Each essay has a different theme, but I hope that you'll find that they are all related to each other in how they spur us on to pursue more of Christ and to walk closely with him. I hesitate to call each section an essay because essays sound so boring and structured. But talking about our life pursuing God really should be exciting and full of life, and I hope I have captured this latter experience rather than the former.

Daniel Bartlett

I'd like to thank my dad who constantly encouraged me to format this into a book and who believed that I could do it. I'd like to thank my editor who wishes to remain anonymous and my wife for designing the book cover and for always being willing to read and comment on anything new that I write. And finally, a big thank you to Dan Born and Cameron Hosmer for reading through the initial draft of this book and giving me invaluable feedback.

May the Lord bless you in your pursuit of him.

THE GREATEST

COMMANDMENT

"Jesus answered, 'The most important is, "Hear, O Israel: The Lord our God, the Lord is one. And you shall love the Lord your God with all your heart and with all your soul and with all your mind and with all your strength." -Mark 12:29

If you were to ask God what the most important thing you could be doing in your life

Daniel Bartlett

right now is, what do you think he would say? Getting more education? Being faithful at work? Working on career advancement? Serving the poor in your community? Taking care of your family? Loving those around you? Taking a vacation? Putting more money into retirement?

Well, a man once did ask God this question, and what was his answer? The most important thing you can be doing with your life right now is loving God with all of your heart, soul, mind, and strength. Yeah, yeah, yeah. Got that one in the bag. I'm a Christian so of course I love God. What's next?

For years this has been my mindset. Jesus spends so much time talking about the second greatest commandment of loving our neighbors that I never gave much thought to the greatest commandment. Until a year ago, I never stopped and asked myself, "Am I loving God with ALL my heart, soul, mind, and strength?" I just assumed I was.

First I needed to correct an error in my understanding of what love Jesus was talking about. I subconsciously thought of loving God as feeling a great fondness for him or a great liking or even devotion. I thought of it only as a feeling. But if you stop and think about it, when Jesus talks about loving your neighbor as yourself, it's all about action. The parable of the Good Samaritan is all about action and how the Samaritan loves the Jewish man. It's not about two cultural enemies sitting around feeling affection for one another.

This is what John is getting at in his letter. "Little children, let us not love in word or talk but in deed and in truth" (1 John 3:18).

Don't get me wrong; love is a feeling, and you can love someone by feeling a great fondness or much affection toward them. But love also expresses itself in action.

This past year month after month the Lord took me through what it looks like to love him with each one of these conditions: heart, soul, mind, and strength. And I'd like to share briefly what I learned about each one.

First was heart. And the thing that was impressed upon me was this statement by Jesus: "Where your treasure is there your heart will be also" (Luke 12:34). Now, I've always thought about treasure as my prized possessions, like a child having a secret stash of goods under their bed in a special box. So I had interpreted Jesus' statement as to not have any prized possessions here on earth. But that is really not what Jesus is saying. In Luke 12 a man comes to Jesus and asks Jesus to tell his brother to stop hogging their inheritance. Instead of sympathizing with this poor man, Jesus calls him out and says, "Take care, and be on your guard against all covetousness, for one's life does not consist in the abundance of his possessions" (Luke 12:15). Jesus then tells a parable of a man who had a bunch of crops and then built big barns to store them up but then died before getting to enjoy all his stuff. He then tells his disciples not to pursue or worry about food, clothing, or daily needs. God will provide for everything you need. Seek first his kingdom. Store up your treasures in heaven. He then says this statement about heart.

Here was my take away. Our heart or love and affections are unavoidably linked to our possessions and what we store up in abundance. Our heart will be with what we store up and pursue. That might be money, crops, investment shares, Legos, frisbee golf discs, home space, education, video game achievements, career advancement, etc. The things God provides for us we are to be generous with and enjoy. But it is an unavoidable fact that our heart will be bound to what we store up, collect, and pursue. We have the choice to direct that either toward the world or toward God and his kingdom.

So God impressed upon me that if I am to truly love him with ALL my heart. I must direct all my pursuits and affections toward him and his kingdom, and I must be very intentional about all my stuff. Being an American has led to a passive storing up of possessions. And this leads to my heart being earthbound. Christmas, birthdays, and the abundance of things to store up and pursue means that I must discipline myself to set limits to what I can own and to be generous when I have way too much stuff.

One practical example of what this teaching led to is in my board games. Over the years I collected probably about thirty board games. I only played maybe two or three regularly. But I found myself loving my board games. I would stare fondly at them on the shelf. I felt secure when I thought about them. I had a strong desire to play board games whenever the opportunity arose, not just to spend time with people but in order to spend time with the board games. Most of those board games saw little to no use, but I loved them. And I always wanted more. My heart was bound to them. But Jesus' teaching on heart led me to give away or donate all but a handful of those board games (the ones we'd actually play when company came over) and to stop buying new ones.

And what happened? I suddenly didn't care about board games very much. I didn't feel an urge to always play them. They were nice when we were bored or wanted something to do with company while we talked. But I didn't need to play them anymore. I didn't think about them regularly. The few I had sat fondly on my shelf, but they actually saw use and added real value to my life. I was able to enjoy them as God's gift to me and not as a worldly pursuit. Most importantly I found my heart freed up. I suddenly had more mental space and affections to direct elsewhere.

Next this happened to my Lego collection and then my video games, then clothes, movies, education, career, and books. Each time I surrendered these things my heart was more free to direct elsewhere. The little that remained I was able to enjoy even more as God's gift to me. This has also led to contentment in each of these areas instead of the constant need for more.

Now, it is important to point out that as I gave up my treasures my heart became more free to direct elsewhere. My heart didn't automatically begin to love God more. There was temptation to just direct that freed-up space into some other worldly pursuit. I had to be intentional about directing that freed-up love toward God.

But when I did focus my freed up time, attention, and love toward God and toward spending time with him without all the distracted loves pulling at my heart, I found such love, peace, and contentment in him. No other pursuit could compare with what I found in God's presence. I could say with the psalmist, "Your love is better than life" and, "In your presence there is fullness of joy; at your right hand are pleasures forevermore" (Psalm 63:3, 16:11).

God wants us to love him with ALL our heart, not just some of it. "You will seek me and find me, when you seek me with all your heart" (Jeremiah 29:13). We cannot collect and chase after the things of this world and love God with all our heart. Directing our whole heart toward God is the greatest thing we can be doing right now. God doesn't want our divided love; he wants it all.

Next God took me through soul. In Greek the word for soul means your life or your self. It's your identity and who you are. It's your life. God wants us to love him with our complete self. I think the implications of this statement are deep, and I know I have only played in the shallows. But here is what the Lord impressed upon me.

I am to love him with my whole life. Everything is on the table: where I live, where I work, who I spend time with, how I view myself, and what I invest my time and energy in. It took a long time, but the Lord destroyed my desire and deep need to have a career or find my identity in a job. I had to surrender my pursuit of education that was fueled by a desire to develop my identity and to have a place in this world. I had to surrender my community and family relationships for a time. God wanted all of me. He desired my whole self to be in total dependence on him.

All In

Next God took me through mind. This one is a doozy. My mind is so full of junk, sin, and distractions. First, it's hard for my mind to be full of anything except constant distraction let alone God. Now, I don't have any form of social media; I don't have friends that text me more than once a month; I'm not interested in sports or news updates; the only video games that I have have been especially chosen for their non addictive qualities; I have strict rules about buying things; I don't spend time surfing the web; I have all notifications disabled; but my phone still is a constant little voice in my ear, "Pick me up! Look at me! Pay attention to me!" Guess I'm checking the weather or checking to see if I got a new email in the past three minutes.

Daniel Bartlett

We live in a world designed for mental distraction. The smartphone is just one example of this. How can I love God with my mind in a world where I have zero mental attention to spare? In response to this, God taught me about Sabbath and gave me a space (a day each week) to take a break from all the noise. It's a day where my phone is locked away, where the internet and TV are off limits, and where busy plans are not allowed. In other words God gave me a space for my mind to begin to free itself up from the constant distraction of this world. And what did I find in my mind? Oh boy. Years and years of unprocessed content, feelings, hurts, desires, memories, and thousands of random scenes from movies I never had space to think about. Seriously, when I sat down to pray

All In

I would just end up thinking about random Star Trek episodes or Binky from Arthur (where'd he come from?).

God wants all of our mind, not just some of it. We can't stuff our minds full of entertainment and distraction and love God with ALL our minds. For most of us getting to the place of enough mental freedom to redirect toward God is going to take a huge amount of intentionality, sacrifice, and time: time spent with God in his word and in prayer processing our unhealthy mental habits and all the stuff stored away in our brains.

Jesus told his disciples to abide in him and to have his words abide in them. This is the key to bearing fruit. Our world of distraction is designed so that this won't happen. If we are to stand against the schemes of the devil, we need to not be people of distraction and full of mental trash. We need to be people full of Jesus and of his word. People who love God with ALL our minds.

Finally, God took me through strength. What in the world does it mean to love God with my body? In the West we are ironically so focused on interacting with God through our minds that loving God with my body is a foreign concept to me. But in short here is what I now understand it to mean.

First, we are to honor God in our work. We are to do our work as though working for God rather than our employers. We are to work hard and work well. This is loving God with our strength.

All In

It is also loving God as a temple of the Holy Spirit. We are embodied people that God has chosen to dwell in. We need to take care of and honor our bodies.

Loving God with our bodies also means interacting with God through physical spiritual practices and not just mental ones. This looks like fasting: getting in touch with God's Spirit and expressing our hunger for God through our bodies. It looks like worshiping God through raised hands and dancing. It looks like spending time with God while actually physically alone. It looks like appropriate feasting. It looks like physical practices like Sabbath.

We aren't just brains on a stick. God has created us as holistic beings with a body, mind, and spirit. He created us with the intent that we would interact with him with our whole self. Our future vision of perfection is not a disembodied experience. Jesus stands at the right hand of God at this very moment in a glorified human body. We will live forever on the new earth in risen bodies. Loving God with our bodies matters to God.

To be honest, loving God with my body is foreign to me and a bit hard for me to incorporate into my walk with God. But over the past year beginning to practice this has been super transformational and the means through which I have encountered God in whole new ways.

Jesus said that the most important thing we can be doing right now is loving God with ALL our heart, soul, mind, and strength. Let us strive with all we are to do so.

Daniel Bartlett

BEARING FRUIT

"By this my Father is glorified that you bear much fruit and so prove to be my disciples." -John 15:8

The more I pursue Jesus, the more I feel like I'm missing something. I look at Jesus, his disciples, and Jesus' teachings, and then I look at my own life. And there is a disconnect. Jesus made some pretty bold statements and promises to his disciples. "Truly, truly, I say to you, whoever believes in me will also do the works that I do;

greater works than these will he do, because I am going to the Father" (John 14:12).

That's a pretty bold statement! In case you didn't know, Jesus did some pretty crazy stuff: walking on water, turning water to wine, feeding thousands with a tiny amount of food. . . oh, and healing people of lifetime infirmities, casting out demons, fasting forty days (I consider that pretty extraordinary), and much more. But Jesus casually drops that whoever believes in him will do all that. Oh, and actually we'll do greater stuff than that because walking on water isn't great enough.

Here's another one. "If you abide in me, and my words abide in you, ask whatever you wish, and it will be done for you. By this my Father is glorified, that you bear much fruit and so prove to be my disciples" (John 15:7-8). Huh. Jesus doesn't say, "Pray. God will always answer you. Sometimes the answer will just be, 'No.'" He says, "Ask whatever you want. It will be done for you." He actually says that he wants this to happen because it brings glory to God. Jesus and the Father aren't opposing our prayers. They want our prayers to happen. They get glory from answering them.

It's statements like these that make me feel like I'm missing something. Raised anyone from the dead recently? Yeah, me neither. Walked on water or fed thousands with one box of cereal and a half gallon of milk? Nope, not me. Had every prayer answered by God with a resounding, yes! Hmm... I stopped praying bold prayers a while ago because I was tired of disappointment.

Well, maybe I'm just missing something. Jesus did put the condition of abiding in him as a prerequisite for answering whatever we ask. Maybe I'm not abiding in him good enough? Maybe I can learn from someone else? Except, when I look around, I don't see anyone else doing these things either. Was Jesus lying? In the book of Acts it seems like his disciples lived out these promises. They healed people. They raised people from the dead. They did pretty extraordinary things. Maybe the promises just applied to the first century Christians? Maybe "whoever" doesn't mean me? Maybe the whole American church that I've been exposed to is just composed of spiritual wimps? Maybe I am a spiritual wimp? Do I not really abide in or believe in Jesus?

All In

When I read these promises of Jesus, I have a deep desire for more of God. Despite my questions and occasional doubts, I am convinced that Jesus' promises are true and apply to all of his disciples. There is so much more to God and this Christian life that I am convinced that I am missing out on. Anyone else have some fomo? I want to go deeper. I feel a tugging need and deep hunger to know more of who God is, to abide more and more in Jesus.

But how? I think the devil has played me. And if you're like me, he may be getting to you too. Here's what I mean by that. During his life on earth, Jesus told a parable of a man who went to sow some seed. This man chucked seed all over the place: on the rocks, on the paths, in the thorns, and (finally) on some good soil. Jesus explained to his disciples that the seed is comparable to how people receive his message. I want to focus on the last two places of seed fall, the thorns and good soil, because the other seeds die, but these don't.

In most church sermons I think it is assumed that Christians are either the sower in the parable or the good soil. But it's interesting that the seed that falls among the thorns doesn't actually die. There are still plants there. Jesus only says, "Their fruit does not mature" (Luke 8:14). The thorns choke those plants, and they have unripe fruit.

Why do I say all this? Well, I have a suspicion that for a long time I've been the plant in the thorns. I have a suspicion that much of the

American Church is growing in the thorns. I think the devil has created a Christian environment in America that makes growing among the thorns normal. And this makes our fruit "not mature." The devil has tricked us, and this is why there is a disconnect between the life Jesus lays out for us and the life we are living.

Why do I think this? Well, let's look at how Jesus describes these plants. "And as for the seed that fell among the thorns, they are those who hear, but as they go on their way they are choked by the cares and riches and pleasures of life, and their fruit does not mature" (John 8:14). The cares and riches and pleasures of life–these things can be a hindrance to living a fruitful life.

First, to expel the elephant in the room, Jesus doesn't say to live in a monastic society with no money or earthly possessions completely cut off from any cares in life; oh, and eat stale bread and abstain from anything that brings you pleasure. That is not what Jesus is saying. God created us to delight in him, to create, and to enjoy the good things in creation. Before his death Jesus told his disciples to take a money bag with them acknowledging that they need money to survive in the world. And Jesus told his disciples that in this world they would have trouble (or cares). Jesus is not creating a list of vices here.

So what is Jesus saying? Money, pleasure, and life's daily burdens can hinder the work of the gospel in our lives. First, let's look at money.

All In

Someone in the crowd said to him, "Teacher, tell my brother to divide the inheritance with me." But he said to him, "Man, who made me a judge or arbitrator over you?" And he said to them, "Take care, and be on your guard against all covetousness, for one's life does not consist in the abundance of his possessions." And he told them a parable, saying, "The land of a rich man produced plentifully, and he thought to himself, 'What shall I do, for I have nowhere to store my crops?' And he said, 'I will do this: I will tear down my barns and build larger ones, and there I will store all my grain and my goods. And I will say to my soul, "Soul, you have ample goods laid up for many years; relax, eat, drink, be merry."' But God said to him, 'Fool! This night your soul is required of you, and the things you have prepared, whose will they be?' So is the one who lays up treasure for himself and is not rich toward God." And he said to his disciples, "Therefore I tell you, do not be anxious about your life, what you will eat, nor about your body, what you will put on. For life is more than food, and the body more than clothing. Consider the ravens: they neither sow nor reap, they have neither storehouse nor barn, and yet God feeds them. Of how much more value are you than the birds! And which of you by being anxious can add a single hour to his span of life? If then you are not able to do as small a thing as that, why are you anxious about the rest? Consider the lilies, how they grow: they neither toil nor spin, yet I tell you, even Solomon in all his glory was not arrayed like one of these. But if God so clothes the grass, which is alive in the field today, and tomorrow is thrown into the oven, how much more will he clothe you, O you of little faith! And do not seek what you are to eat and what you are to drink, nor be worried. For all the nations of the world seek after these things, and your Father knows that you need them. Instead, seek his kingdom, and these things will be added to you. Fear not, little flock, for it is your Father's good pleasure to give you the kingdom. Sell your possessions, and give to the needy. Provide yourselves with moneybags that do not grow old, with a treasure in the heavens that does not fail, where no thief approaches and no moth destroys. For where your treasure is, there will your heart be also (Luke 12:13-34).

Here Jesus talks about pretty basic needs: food and clothing. His message? The world chases after these things. God knows you need them, and he will provide for you. Invest in following Jesus, and he will take care of you.

Here is my temptation. I need to get a good job that will support me and my family. I need enough money to 1) support our month-to-month expenses, 2) support our spending habits (getting ice cream once in a while, being able to afford presents on birthdays and holidays, being able to go on a vacation once a year, etc.), and 3) be able to put away enough savings for retirement, my kids' college, and fixing things around the house.

If I were a betting man, I would bet my best pencil that after reading that list you thought something along the lines of, "That sounds pretty reasonable!" I think so too. Except there is a snag. This is the priority in my life. Once I have this financial security, then I can do kingdom work. I put more thought and effort into my career or dreaming up a good job than I do into pursuing Jesus.

Jesus' point in the parable of the rich fool is to not focus on accumulating and storing up wealth. Don't even pursue providing for your basic needs. Everyone around you is chasing after these things. "But not you," Jesus says. Seek God's kingdom, and all that you need will be provided for you. Sell your stuff. Give to those who really need it. Build your investment portfolio in heavenly assets not in the stock market or a thriving 401k. Don't focus on storing up or accumulating wealth. Be content with what you have. Don't always be seeking the next better job or the next raise. That's not where life in Jesus lies.

News flash: the devil can offer you a really good job. He offered it to Jesus in the wilderness. "And the devil took him up and showed him all the kingdoms of the world in a moment of time, and said to him, 'To you I will give all this authority and their glory, for it has been delivered to me, and I give it to whom I will. If you, then, will worship me, it will all be yours" (Luke 4:5-7). Satan is all for upward mobility as long as it costs our souls.

I need to repeat it once more. Jesus recognizes that we need money to live in the world. But he also recognizes that the pursuit of and the desire for money leads to slavery to this world. I believe that for Jesus the focus is the key. What is your focus on? Where's the bullseye that you're trying to hit? Is it more of God and his kingdom in your life and the life of those around you? Or is it your career and money? You need to work, but is

Daniel Bartlett

that the focus of your pursuits? Do you trust God to provide for you? What if he calls you into a place of financial insecurity? Will you follow?

I think that as American Christians many of us have bought into a narrative that is contrary to Jesus' teachings and totally in line with the teachings of our culture. For example I think most Christian parents would say that all that they want for the child is for them to follow Jesus. But I also think most Christian parents invest more in and put more pressure on their child's education and future. If you grew up in a Christian home in America, I think there's a good chance this was ingrained in you. We say one thing but communicate another. This is the narrative we have adopted as the American Church: the pursuit of a stable career comes first. It is ingrained in us. We have bought into our culture's pursuit of money. And just like the plant among thorns it is choking us and making us unfruitful.

As a last, somewhat aside point concerning the pursuit of financial security, throughout my life when I read this teaching of Jesus, I have been tempted to combine my pursuit of a career with seeking God's kingdom by working for different ministries. I think others might fall into this temptation too. I think this is why many might see certain professions as inherently more holy while others as secular. I don't think this divide exists. During my lifetime I have worked at a Christian university and at a mission organization as a "missionary." I think other "holy" professions where we view career and kingdom to be combined are working at a church or a Christian non-profit. These are good things to work for, but also dangerous, because suddenly pursuing money and Jesus seem to become synonymous. We can put our effort into financial security and the kingdom at the same time. As the great Admiral Ackbar once said, "It's a trap!" These organizations are not the same as the kingdom, and working for them does not inherently mean seeking God's kingdom. One can be seeking God's kingdom and pursuing Jesus working at Taco Bell just as well as working for the International Missions Board or for World Vision.

Second, let's look at the pleasures of life.

Do not love the world or the things in the world. If anyone loves the world, the love of the Father is not in him. For all that is in the world—the desires of the flesh and the desires of the eyes and the pride of life— is not from the Father but is from the world. And the world is passing away along with its desires, but whoever does the will of God abides forever (1 John 2:15-17).

God made us in his image. Because of this we are designed to be little creators imitating our Father. We are also designed to delight in what we've created and in what God has created. "And God saw everything that he had made, and behold, it was very good" (Genesis 1:31). Like God, after creating we can step back and delight in it and say,

49

"That is really good." This idea of delighting in good, beautiful things is ingrained in our nature, put there by God himself. God designed us to enjoy many things: good food, a beautiful sunset, an invigorating game of pickup basketball, quilting, Lego bricks, a really well made film, and among other things God himself.

If God made us for pleasure, how can we be choked by it? Why is it a bad thing? Before we dive into this, I need to define two words that John uses in the passage above: world and flesh.

Words have multiple meanings. I think we all know this. Bowl can mean a thing I eat my cereal out of, or it can mean the action of throwing a heavy ball down a lane toward nine pins. Crane, ball, spike, and duck are other words with two or three meanings. The word in Greek translated as world has multiple meanings in the New Testament. It can mean the physical world, the earth itself such as in Acts 17:24. It can mean the people in the world, the populated world such as in John 3:16. Or it can mean something like the systems, values, and practices of secular society which are ultimately under the reign of Satan. This third definition is what John is referring to when he talks about the world.

Next the flesh. The flesh is also commonly used in three different ways. It can simply refer to the physical body such as in 1 Corinthians 6:16. It can refer to peoples or ethnic groups such as in 1 Peter 1:24. For the last meaning I find the definition by pastor John Mark Comer helpful.

"The animalistic cravings of our body apart from God."[2] Again, this third definition is what John is referring to.

So when John says, "Do not love the world or the things in the world," he is not saying, "Don't love your fellow earthlings" nor "Despise the beautiful view of that waterfall." John is taking a stand against the influence of the devil on our society. Satan has lost. His kingdom will pass away along with everything that his kingdom has created. Do not love it. Do not delight in it. Like my Greek professor once said, "The things of this world are like a receding tide. If we cling onto them, we will be swept away with them." In this sense, the pleasures of this world are evil, and they are to be resisted, not enjoyed.

All In

So God created us for pleasure and delight. But Satan has got his hands all over God's good earth and warped it into his evil designs. So how are we as Christians supposed to know what is good and right to delight in and what is to be rejected?

I cannot answer that for you. I think Satan has his hands all over what we end up creating, and he is crafty about how he influences us. Also, in the corrupted part of our flesh, we eagerly contribute to the messed up pleasures of the world.

Also, I think that what Satan uses changes over time. At one time card playing and ballroom dancing were key instruments of the devil. They held honored places in his schemes to lead people away from Christ and into his world of pleasures. And many viewed these things as so evil to be utterly repulsive. Now, we laugh at those views. Ballroom dancing and card playing are so tame that it often seems ridiculous to even think about them leading anyone away from Jesus. I think that the devil moved on. He is instead focusing his energies elsewhere. Movies? Social media? Video games? Sports? I do not know. I think there are kingdom people in these sectors of life focused on using their image-bearing creativity to create things that are good, beautiful, and true, things to be enjoyed and delighted in. I also think that there are kingdom people interacting with these things in redemptive ways. But I think that Satan is crafty and has much influence in what we look to for entertainment.

So what are we to do? How are we to know where the line is? I think we must take a line from Paul here. "Do not be conformed to this world, but be transformed by the renewal of your mind, that by testing you may discern what is the will of God, what is good and acceptable and perfect" (Romans 12:2). We must be people who abide in Christ and are transformed into his likeness. We must be people who are not conformed to the world. If this is the case, then we will be able to test and know what is good, acceptable, and perfect, interacting with certain pleasures in ways that are good, right, and redeeming and knowing what to reject as dishonoring to God.

If we are not people who abide constantly in Christ and are not transformed into his likeness, if we have the sneaking suspicion that we may in some areas of our lives be conformed to the sinful culture around us, then I would say two things. First, begin to abide in Christ regularly. Spend as much free time as you can in Bible study, Christian community, worship, and prayer. Second, begin to cut off or limit anything you think is worldly. Don't take any chances. "If your right eye causes you to sin, tear it out and throw it away. For it is better that you lose one of your members than that your whole body be thrown into hell. And if your right hand causes you to sin, cut it off and throw it away. For it is better that you lose one of your members than that your whole body go into hell" (Matthew

5:29-30). As you begin to make space to be transformed into Christ's likeness and cut away your worldly loves, you will begin to be able to tell what was good and able to be redeemed and what was not. Once this testing is complete, you can take up again what was good and leave alone what was not.

So besides pleasure as simply enjoying what has been corrupted by the world, why does Jesus list pleasure as a hindrance to our fruitful life in him? Remember, the point of all that we have been discussing is to try to figure out how to live a full abundant life in Jesus in full alignment with his teachings and promises. It is the difference between a life of bearing fruit a hundred fold with patience versus living a choked life with unripe fruit. If you do not hunger for an abundant life in Jesus, please ignore all that I am saying.

That being said, I think another danger of pleasure is having too much of a good thing. "My son, eat honey, for it is good, and the drippings of the honeycomb are sweet to your taste" (Proverbs 24:13). "If you have found honey, eat only enough for you, lest you have your fill of it and vomit it" (Proverbs 25:16). I used the example of building Legos earlier to describe a way we are made in the image of God, to create and delight in our creation. I think this is good. Now, let's suppose building Legos became my thing, my obsession. I spent a large amount of money each year on new Lego sets. My house was crowded with Legos on shelves, in boxes, everywhere! Legos were what I thought about all the time and invested my life in. I just always had to have the newest, best Lego.

This is a good thing gone bad. I have taken a legitimate delight and pleasure, a way I reflect God's image, and warped it into something unhealthy and toxic. This is what the enemy does, and in our sinful flesh, we are prone to do it too.

This has been happening throughout history. God created so many things to be good, but we end up worshiping creation rather than the creator. In our present culture, we take the pleasure God created to be good, and we worship it. Food is a good example of this, but it can be any number of things. Our addiction to pleasure is another way it has gone bad, and it will choke any fruit from our lives.

Finally, I think the way we worship pleasure itself is included in Jesus' critique of it. In America, we live for pleasure. We live for that next binge session of that TV series. We feast constantly for the pleasure it brings us. Why would we ever have a drab, boring meal? For our body's health? Pish posh, if eating is not pleasurable, it is hardly worth it. We work so that we can buy more and more pleasure whether in things or in experiences. The goal and purpose of our lives is to get through life with as little discomfort as possible and as much pleasure as possible. This is the American dream, and much of our American Christianity has been conformed to it.

So when Jesus talks about the seed of the gospel being choked by the pleasures of life, I believe all of this is what he means. The American church has been largely influenced by our pleasure loving culture, and this is a reason why we show so little fruit and have such a disconnect between our lives and the life Jesus promises for his disciples.

Finally, Jesus mentions the cares of life.

As I said earlier, we all have cares in life. Jesus told his disciples that they would have much trouble in the world. They would be persecuted, executed, and brought before judges. The Apostles were no strangers to hardships and needs.

Three times I was beaten with rods. Once I was stoned. Three times I was shipwrecked; a night and a day I was adrift at sea; on frequent journeys, in danger from rivers, danger from robbers, danger from my own people, danger from Gentiles, danger in the city, danger in the wilderness, danger at sea, danger from false brothers; in toil and hardship, through many a sleepless night, in hunger and thirst, often without food, in cold and exposure. And, apart from other things, there is the daily pressure on me of my anxiety for all the churches (2 Corinthians 11:25-29).

(*Mic drop from Paul). One of my biggest concerns is worrying if I'll have money left over to put in my 401k, so Paul definitely wins the more cares list.

So, going back to the issue at hand, how are cares choking out the fruit of the gospel in our lives? Why are cares a hindrance to us following

Jesus? Obviously, Jesus and his disciples had cares in life. They needed to eat. They needed clothes on their backs. Many had families to support and to take care of. Many of them were social outcasts. They had plenty of trouble to get along with. So how did they bear so much fruit? What's the difference between them and us?

Again, I think perspective and attitude make or break whether cares are hindering our growth here. It's about focus. "If then you have been raised with Christ, seek the things that are above, where Christ is, seated at the right hand of God. Set your minds on things that are above, not on things that are on the earth" (Colossians 3:1-2). As Christians we are called to set our gaze on things above not on things on earth. Of course we still have dealings with the world, but that is to not be what consumes our time, goals, and attention.

Let me re-quote a short portion of teaching from Jesus. "And do not seek what you are to eat and what you are to drink, nor be worried. For all the nations of the world seek after these things, and your Father knows that you need them. Instead, seek his kingdom, and these things will be added to you" (Luke 12:29-31). Eating and drinking and clothing are pretty basic needs, but Jesus says don't even worry about or seek after obtaining these things. Don't give your focus or attention to providing for yourself. Wow. That's a bold statement. The nations devote themselves to these things: getting an education, a good job, a retirement plan, a bigger house, good health insurance, etc. But Jesus says not his followers. They are to give their attention and energies to something greater.

This is honestly hard for me to stomach. This is a bold statement that Jesus makes. And we must either accept it and commit to living this way of life as his disciples or say, "No thanks" to Jesus' offer to follow him. "Enter by the narrow gate. For the gate is wide and the way is easy that leads to destruction, and those who enter by it are many. For the gate is narrow and the way is hard that leads to life, and those who find it are few" (Matthew 7:13-14). I'm not sure I signed up for this.

I think it would be easy to lump in much of the American Church into Jesus' statement. "The

Daniel Bartlett

nations of the world and my followers in America seek after these things..." Our Christian culture makes it not only normal but good to focus on what Jesus says specifically not to focus on. And I believe this is why we are living choked, unfruitful lives.

Again, I must make some clarification here. We as Christians are commanded to earn our own living. "If anyone is not willing to work, let him not eat. For we hear that some among you walk in idleness, not busy at work, but busybodies. Now such persons we command and encourage in the Lord Jesus Christ to do their work quietly and to earn their own living" (2 Thessalonians 3:10-12). Idleness is not a Christian virtue. We are commanded to work and take care of our families.

All In

God knows we need to do this, and he will provide a way if only we will devote our attention to him. Again, focus, attention, seeking, heart, and goals are what are the keys to Jesus' teachings.

"I know how to be brought low, and I know how to abound. In any and every circumstance, I have learned the secret of facing plenty and hunger, abundance and need. I can do all these through him who strengthens me" (Philippians 4:12-13).

To be honest, this is the one that has got me the most. Riches I heed not, and I'm a bit of a monk at heart, so I find rejecting pleasures kind of fun. But the cares of life trap me again and again and lead me down into a spiral. Up until now we have used food, clothing, and providing as examples of cares because that is what Jesus talks about and because these are such basic needs that they get to the heart of how dependent Jesus expects us to be on God. But I think there is a lot more that we can qualify as cares in our lives.

I have realized that at the time of writing this I am living a double life. Half of my life in utter devotion to Jesus and half invested in the cares of life. The weight of this life has gotten to me, and I have chosen to bear it. One of my primary concerns at the moment is finding a career and providing for my family. Not a bad thing, but it has begun to consume me. My focus and attention have been on it. I have been among the number who "seek after these things." I have felt in my heart a willingness to compromise in my values in order to provide for my family. If Satan offered me a really good job, I'd be tempted to take it.

A few months ago I was working a high intensity job, and every day I came home mentally and physically exhausted. This resulted in a different form of compromise to the cares of life: self-care. I would come home, eat unhealthily, and lose myself in a good book or TV show. I had gotten to the point in my life where I could not fathom living my life without my books or a movie once in a while. I needed these things to take care of myself. I had to have them to live. My identity became wrapped up in them.

We talked earlier about pleasures and their dangers and virtues. But here we have something different. The cares of life (working a stressful job) led me to ground my focus on earthly things and not on things above. I had to take care of myself, but instead of looking up, I looked further down. God desires to give us rest after work. He commands it for his people in the forms of sabbath and a sabbatical year. But I was looking for leisure after toil not rest after work.[3] This form of self-care was me giving into the cares of this world.

All of this resulted in a lack of fruit in that season of my own life. When I was attentive, I could feel the Spirit being choked within me. I still did all of my regular spiritual practices. I still heard from God regularly. But I also felt his work being hindered in my life. I also felt myself compromising. Honoring God was a priority in my life. My spirit was deeply grieved whenever I heard anyone dishonor or make light of God, and I rejected any form of creative work that dishonored him. But as in the area of work, I had compromised. Remember, we are designed to create and delight in creation, but when that creation dishonors God, we are to not delight in it. I had found myself delighting in movies and books that dishonor God and celebrate or make light of sin. These books spit in God's face, and I called them good. I not only called them good, but I could not imagine getting by in life without them. Focusing on the cares of life had driven me to this compromise and position of unfruitfulness.

We began this essay by looking at Jesus' promises to his disciples. They would do greater things than him. They would have every prayer answered. They would be full of fruit. And we asked the question of why we don't experience this spiritual power and fruit. We then looked at the teaching of Jesus about how riches, pleasure, and cares will choke one's life and make it unfruitful. The pursuit of and compromise to these things are the norm in American Christianity. We live as an unfruitful people, not the fruitful crops that Jesus describes. Jesus' teachings demand a change in our lives. Will we continue as his disciples? Or will we choose the world?

All In

A SABBATH REST

"Remember the Sabbath day, to keep it holy. Six days you shall labor, and do all your work, but the seventh day is a Sabbath to the Lord your God. On it you shall not do any work, you, or your son, or your daughter, your male servant, or your female servant, or your livestock, or the sojourner who is within your gates. For in six days the Lord made heaven and earth, the sea, and all that is in them, and rested on the seventh

day. Therefore the Lord blessed the Sabbath day and made it holy." -Exodus 20:8-12

Rest as an act of worship. A whole day each week set apart to the Lord. A holy gift given to us by God. This is the Sabbath. We live in a restless world, and our hearts cry out for rest and peace. But for some reason many of us are resistant to the idea of Sabbath. In some ways we are repulsed by it. We are unable to cease from work, activity, and doped up pleasure. I have been personally practicing the Sabbath for seven years now. And in that time I have found that some Christ followers around me are hostilely resistant to the idea of a Sabbath rest. In American culture where productivity is so highly valued, refusing to be productive seems wrong, maybe even sinful.

But these people do not realize what the psalmist found. "Blessed are those whose way is blameless, who walk in the law of the LORD" (Psalm 119:1)! I have experienced such rich benefits in observing the Sabbath. It is among the most formative spiritual practices of my life. And the rest and the peace of mind and body that I have received have totally transformed the way I live. It is this gift that I want to share with you.

In God's perfect vision of society, he envisioned a day of rest. A day set apart to him when all work and striving ceased. And if we're honest, this is what we long for. We desperately need rest for our minds, bodies, and souls. We live in a go-go world where our attention is under attack from a thousand directions. In our hearts we long for stillness, peace, and rest.

God set this pattern of six and one in creation. Six days of work, then one of rest. And then as he set the ground rules for his people in his vision of how society should work, he told his people to follow this pattern. Work six days and then rest. Set apart one day where no one does any work, not you, not your children, not your servants, not your animals, not the people outside your community, nobody. Do not rest at the expense of others. This is God's vision.

Why is our natural reaction to be resistant to it? Well, one reason is that there is a human tendency in us all to overdo things. This is what the Pharisees did. They took God's good command and added a thousand rules to it, turning a good gift into a hard burden. And this is the picture we capture when Jesus comes on the scene in the Gospels. We see Jesus rebuke over and over again the way that the Pharisees practiced the Sabbath and burdened others with their rules.

Jesus and the disciples snack on the sabbath by plucking grain off of plants as they stroll. "Work!!" the Pharisees cry. Jesus heals a man of lameness (by healing his legs not by giving him a pair of sunglasses) and has him carry his mat home. "Work!!" the Pharisees cry. Jesus heals a man's arm. "Work!!" the Pharisees cry!

The Pharisees had fallen into the common trap of overdoing a thing. They added to God's rules and became obsessed with the rules they made. Jesus' message on the Sabbath was, "The Son of Man is Lord of the Sabbath" and, "It is lawful to do good on the Sabbath" (Matthew 12:8,12). Jesus is the one who gets to define what is lawful or not on the Sabbath. He is the one who set it in motion, and he gets to define its terms.

I believe we have three things that turn us against the Sabbath today. First, I think our forefathers fell into the same trap as the Pharisees. Please realize that Christians have been practicing the Sabbath for the past two thousand years. It is only since about the 1960s that a shift took place and most Christians threw the Sabbath out of their spiritual lives. But when I picture the Sabbath of the 1800s and 1900s, I picture children sitting on hard benches, not allowed to play or have fun, only allowed to sit quietly and listen to someone read the Bible. I believe many of our forefathers went a bit overboard in their practice of the Sabbath and in the making of extraneous rules and so left a bad taste in the mouth of their children.

Second, we have become conformed to this age. It used to be commonplace in America for everybody to take Sunday off. Almost every place of work in all of America was closed on Sunday. Christians and non-Christians alike had the day off. Churches were the only place with their doors open. Then businesses like 7-Eleven opened, and the culture began to shift and took the American Church right with it.

Daniel Bartlett

Third, when we look at Jesus' teachings on the Sabbath, it looks like Jesus is anti-Sabbath. He's always critiquing it! We take up the chant, "Jesus was against the Sabbath and so am I!" This is a misconception. Jesus is the Lord of the Sabbath. He is the one who set it in place. He is not against the Sabbath; he was against the hypocrisy of the Pharisees and the burdensome rules that the Pharisees put around the Sabbath.

On this point, let me point out two important points that are relevant to us. First, Jesus and his disciples did practice the Sabbath. He did not teach his disciples to not observe it. Jesus died on the cross the afternoon before the Sabbath started. His disciples then had things to do. They wanted to respect and honor their Lord in his burial. But they rushed things because once evening came, "On the Sabbath, they rested according to the commandment" (Luke 23:56). His disciples were in the habit of observing the Sabbath.

Second, I need to address Paul's teachings on the Sabbath for this is extremely relevant to us. When Gentiles (non Jews) like me started to become Christians, it caused quite a stir. The Apostles had quite a mess sorting out which of the Old Testament laws applied only to Jews and which applied to anyone who wanted to follow Jesus. Circumcision was the hottest topic of the day. Their ruling? Well, the end of the matter is that following the Law doesn't make someone righteous; Jesus does (see Galatians). And their immediate decision about the new Gentile believers was

> *Why are you putting God to the test by placing a yoke on the neck of the disciples that neither our fathers nor we have been able to bear? We believe that we will be saved through the grace of the Lord Jesus, just as they will... We should not trouble those of the Gentiles who turn to God, but should write to them to abstain from the things polluted by idols, and from sexual immorality, and from what has been strangled, and from blood. For from ancient generations Moses has had in every city those who proclaim him, for he*

is read every Sabbath in the synagogues (Acts 15:10-11, 19-21).

In the vein of this teaching, Paul, in his letters to his mixed Jewish and Gentile audiences, makes two comments on the Sabbath. The first is in Romans.

One person esteems one day as better than another, while another esteems all days alike. Each one should be fully convinced in his own mind. The one who observes the day, observes it in honor of the Lord. The one who eats, eats in honor of the Lord, since he gives thanks to God, while the one who abstains, abstains in honor of the Lord and gives thanks to God (Romans 14:5-6).

Paul's main argument here is on eating clean versus unclean food, but he mentions the Sabbath and/or Jewish holidays in passing.

The second instance is more clear and it is in Colossians. "Therefore let no one pass judgment on you in question of food or drink, or with regard to a festival or a new moon or a Sabbath. For these are a shadow of the things to come, but the substance belongs to Christ" (Colossians 2:16-17). Everyone breathe a sigh of relief. Paul is giving us a get out of jail free card. We are not bound to observe the Sabbath. As Gentiles under Christ's new reign, we have tremendous freedom in Christ especially in regards to the Law.

Now let me be clear. Christ did not come to abolish the law but to fulfill it. And now our righteousness before God does not come from following the law but through faith in Christ. And we have freedom because we are no longer enslaved to the impossible standards of rules. In regards to the Sabbath, it belongs to Jesus, and he can give us freedom in this command.

I say this because many of us are trained to reject legalism (which is good), but often we see legalism in every shadow when it isn't actually there (which is bad). Legalism is trying to be righteous before God based on our own works. We are made righteous before God by grace alone through faith alone in Christ alone. It is God's gift to us. But in Christ following God's rules, walking in holiness, and living a righteous life are ways to honor and give glory to God. This we are commanded to do by every New Testament writer. God is worthy of all honor and glory no matter the cost to us.

So if we are trying to be holy to justify ourselves before God, this is legalism and bad. If we are doing everything in our power to walk in step with the Holy Spirit and to live a righteous life in order to glorify God, this is God's command to us and is good. This is somewhat a tangent, but I wanted to make this point. We are not bound to observe the Sabbath. This command will not make us righteous before God. But there are still many good things in God's law. In the law we discover God's heart for us and also much about his nature. Spiritual practices found in scripture like Sabbath, prayer, reading scripture, fasting, and the like do not make us righteous before God, but they are often the means through which we encounter God. There are blessings and benefits found in engaging with these practices.

I have felt it necessary to discuss in length what hinders us from the Sabbath. These things are a wall that many of us hold in our unconscious mind, and they are a hindrance to some of us from experiencing the benefits found in this spiritual practice. But now that we are hopefully through the wall, let us explore the green pastures and quiet waters that lie before us.

Some might say, "If we are not bound to keep the Sabbath, why bother with it?" I repeat myself. In God's PERFECT vision of society, he commanded a Sabbath rest for his people. This should make us turn our heads. We all long for utopia, for the perfect society, and for a fulfilled way of living. What was the reason for God's command? Why did He command a Sabbath?

We live in a restless world. And the cry of our hearts is for peace and rest and refreshment. I think Psalm 23 is a favorite for many of us. "The Lord is my shepherd; I shall not want. He makes me lie down in green pastures. He leads me beside still waters. He restores my soul" (Psalm 23:1-3). What a wonderful vision! Also, some of us are too busy to follow Jesus. We are too caught up in work, relationships, entertainment, and obligations to have a meaningful spiritual life. We need a space of quiet to reconnect with God.

All In

We long for rest. We need it. And God gives it to us through the Sabbath. He gives this gift through a command. We who were raised on Disney don't like commands, but this command is a life giving gift. Now, we have the freedom in Christ to not observe the Sabbath. But my question is why would we not? It's like a child on Christmas choosing to not open one of their presents. I think that this is why early Christians ultimately chose to continue observing the Sabbath even after Paul gave them freedom to ignore the command. They saw it as a good, life giving thing, and they chose to pass it on through the generations.

So for us Sabbath is an invitation into a holy rest. But what does Sabbath look like for us today if we choose to accept this invitation? I view it like an ice cream sundae. As long as we have a few key ingredients, we have the freedom to flavor it however we like. And what are those key ingredients? They are rest from labor and work, solemness, a consistent day, rest not at the expense of others, and rest to the Lord. Let's look at each.

God's command in the Ten Commandments in Exodus and then repeated again in Deuteronomy is that for six days you shall labor and work and on the seventh you shall rest. The seventh day is a day of rest from labor and work. For the Israelites this meant things like not lighting fires to cook, not gathering sticks, and not harvesting crops. Basically not doing any chores or vocational work. Our culture and technology is much different today, but I think that these are the two principles to stick to: no chores and no vocational work.

Again, we have tremendous freedom in Christ, and these will look different for each of us. For example, I love eating good food, but meal planning and cooking feel like chores to me. My family observes the Sabbath on Sunday. So on Friday and Saturday we cook double portions of our dinners, so that we have delicious leftovers to heat up on Sunday. Good food without any planning or cooking. Now, I know some people who love to bake or cook, and for them Sabbath is a time to spend two hours in the kitchen making a gourmet meal from scratch. They find it a restful and refreshing break from the fast paced meals of the busy week.

I always take out the trash, do the dishes, clean the house, and do any other chores I can think of on Saturday, so that I don't have to think about any of that on Sunday. It takes extra work on Saturday, but it is worth it for the total rest on Sabbath. The Jews called this the day of preparation.

Again, we have tremendous freedom in Christ, so what we consider labor may differ for each of us. But we are all invited to rest from all labor one day each week.

In the same way vocational work will differ for each of us. Do you work in manual labor or maintenance? Take a break from lifting stuff or fixing stuff on Sabbath. Save it for the six days. Let it be broken or unmoved for a while. Do you work with social media or on your computer? Turn off your phone and your computer for a day. You know what is work for you. You are invited by God to put it down for a whole day. The Sabbath is a day each week set aside from any work or labor.

As we wrap up this point, I must make a point. Although what we think of as labor and work may be different for each of us, work is still work, even if you enjoy it a bunch. You may love your job. The Sabbath is still a day to take a break from it. You may really love taking out the trash, cleaning, or mowing the lawn. Sabbath is not a day to catch up on household chores, to do the weekly grocery run, or to do whatever you want. It is a day of rest to the Lord.

Now, my dad is a doctor, and as a final point I must address church workers and essential workers. When my dad and I discuss the Sabbath, he often talks about his profession as a doctor and how there are some emergency services that must be available all the time. What if someone has to have a baby on the Sabbath? What if there was a fire? There still needs to be law and order. For my pastor friends "the Sabbath" is the day they work the most. What do we do about all of this?

Here are my thoughts on these things. With the freedom we have in Christ to observe the Sabbath, I think the simple solution is for these people to observe the Sabbath on different days.

All In

Many pastors I know of either observe the Sabbath on Saturdays or on Mondays even though they encourage their congregations to observe the Sabbath on Sundays. Essential workers like doctors and nurses could have a system where half Sabbath on Saturday and the other half on Sunday. Both of those are days that the Sabbath has been historically observed.

Jesus made it clear that it is lawful (under his way of doing things) to do good on the Sabbath. It is lawful to save a life. Also, in the Law the priests working in the temple were allowed to continue working and offering sacrifices on the Sabbath. In fact they were commanded to offer double the sacrifices and work twice as much. Now, they were on three month work rotations so this was only their experience for part of their year. But still work for worship was allowed.

We must now move to our second key ingredient. This past year as I was reading through my Bible a curious phrase kept jumping out at me. "Six days shall work be done, but on the seventh day is a Sabbath of solemn rest, a holy convocation. You shall do no work. It is a Sabbath to the Lord in all your dwelling places" (Leviticus 23:3). Solemn rest. This phrase is repeated over and over again in the Old Testament in connection with the Sabbath. When I first learned about practicing the Sabbath, I learned about it as a day of feasting, delight, and worship. So I was always confused about the solemn bit. It sounds so sad, boring, and depressing. It sounds a bit like sitting on a hard bench having no fun. But this past year I came to understand what is meant by it.

Have you ever spent a whole day watching seven hours of football? At the end of that time do you say, "I feel so rested, refreshed, and ready for a new week!" Have you ever binge watched a TV show, played video games all day, or been to a movie theater? Do you feel rested and refreshed after those experiences or zapped and a bit dead inside?

I recently went with my family to Disney World on vacation. The messaging was that our vacation would be nonstop fun: rides, shops, entertainment, and food. We came back from that trip completely wiped out, tired, grumpy, and irritable. Nothing about it was restful or refreshing. It was fun but not restful.

Here is the point. The Sabbath is to be a day of solemn rest. It is not a day full of fun activities, big parties, entertainment, and games. These things are fun and good, but they are often not restful or refreshing, especially in large quantities. They spike our inner dopamine levels and get our bodies more active and stressed. They don't give us the rest we long for.

So what is the Sabbath full of if not full of fun and entertainment? Like I said, I've learned the Sabbath to be a day of rest, worship, and delight. It is a day for naps and reading a good book with a warm drink. It is a day for a stroll with family members. It is a day for feasting on good food. It is a day to worship God with others. It is a day to delight in creation, watching the birds sing, noticing the color of the trees, watching the grass grow. It is a day to sit in God's presence and just delight in him. It is a day to stop our busy, hurried lives and minds and to be still and know that God is God and we are not.

I must now say that I believe that Sabbath is to be consistent. This is our third point. Again, we have so much freedom in Christ. But this rhythm of six and one is important, so important that God framed creation around it. We are invited into the Sabbath, but once we choose to esteem one day as better than others, I am convinced that we should not be wishy-washy about it.

Daniel Bartlett

My family observes Sabbath from Saturday at sundown to Sunday at sundown. We start Sabbath with a feast and end with sleep. Many pastors and church workers I know observe Sabbath on Saturday, or Friday night through Saturday. The Jews (including Jesus) observed Sabbath from Friday at sundown to Saturday at sundown. I believe that in Christ we have the freedom to observe Sabbath on the day that works best for us, our families, or our church communities. But once we have picked that day, I believe it is important to be consistent and to stand our ground on observing it.

I have known those who are quite flexible about the Sabbath. Once they heard about it, they excitedly set aside a day to observe it. But then something came up the first week. Oh, well, there's always next week. Then something came up again: sports, travel, a special work event. I don't know if they've ever been able to actually practice the Sabbath. I know others who try to move their Sabbath around. One week it's Saturday, the next Monday, the next Thursday. The Sabbath just follows their day off. From my observation this doesn't work either.

God clearly set in motion the rhythm of six and one. It is important. We are creatures of habit and if we either try to move the Sabbath around it will become a sporadic eight and one then nine and one, etc. And if we aren't serious about the Sabbath, things will always come up to keep us from resting. We live in a busy world that demands our attention after all.

Consistently observing the Sabbath is difficult. I have quit my job and lost many job opportunities because I did not have a flexible enough schedule or because I was not willing to let work come into every day of my week. I have been viewed as difficult and unhelpful because of not doing chores or saying no to excessive entertainment. But the rest, refreshment, and richness I have received in Christ has paid for it all tenfold. Jesus said that the path was narrow and the way difficult that leads to life and there would be few on it, and his invitation to the Sabbath is the same.

All In

Next, for our fourth point, God is clear that we are not to rest at the expense of others.

Observe the Sabbath day, to keep it holy, as the LORD your God commanded you. Six days you shall labor and do all your work, but the seventh day is a Sabbath to the LORD your God. On it you shall not do any work, you or your son or your daughter or your male servant or your female servant, or your ox or your donkey or any of your livestock or the sojourner who is within your gates, that your male servant and your female servant may rest as well as you. You shall remember that you were a slave in the land of Egypt, and the LORD God brought you out from there with a mighty hand and an outstretched arm. Therefore the LORD your God commanded you to keep the Sabbath day (Deuteronomy 5:12-15).

In Exodus in Moses' first presentation of the Ten Commandments quoted at the beginning, Moses says that the reason the Israelites should keep the Sabbath is because God made the world in six days and rested on the seventh. He ingrained that rhythm of work and rest into the fabric of creation, and we should follow it. In Deuteronomy, Moses is repeating God's commands to the next generation of Israelites, and he gives a different reason to remember the Sabbath: because you were slaves in Egypt. In other words, "Remember how you were driven by Pharaoh? Remember how you had to work nonstop? Remember how your parents had to make bricks with no straw? Remember how they were driven to utter exhaustion seven days a week under unreasonable demands? Don't ever return to that. And don't you ever become like Pharaoh! Give every living thing in your community a day of rest: your children, servants, and animals."

The command for Sabbath is not a command to rest at the expense of others. It is not a day for us to skive off while others pick up the slack. It is a day of communal rest.

So what does this look like for us today? Before we answer that question, I need to tell you one more story.

Nehemiah: a radical dude with a passion for following God. Profession: cupbearer to the king of Babylon. Life's work: rebuilding the wall of Jerusalem. Timeline: lived during the Jews' exile in Babylon and during their return to Jerusalem. Now that we have Nehemiah's bio let's look at a specific instance of his life concerning the Sabbath. The wall of Jerusalem has been rebuilt. Leadership has been re-established in Jerusalem. And Nehemiah is taking a short vacation from the palace in Babylon to visit the city and see how things are going. And what does he find?

> *In those days I saw in Judah people treading winepresses on the Sabbath, and bringing in heaps of grain and loading them on donkeys, and also wine, grapes,*

figs, and all kinds of loads, which they brought into Jerusalem on the Sabbath day. And I warned them on the day when they sold food. Tyrians also, who lived in the city, brought in fish and all kinds of goods and sold them on the Sabbath to the people of Judah, in Jerusalem itself! Then I confronted the nobles of Judah and said to them, "What is this evil thing that you are doing, profaning the Sabbath day? Did not your fathers act in this way, and did not our God bring all this disaster on us and on this city? Now you are bringing more wrath on Israel by profaning the Sabbath." As soon as it began to grow dark at the gates of Jerusalem before the Sabbath, I commanded that the doors should be shut and gave orders that they should not be opened until after the Sabbath. And I stationed some of my servants at the gates, that no load might be brought in on the Sabbath day. Then the merchants and sellers of all kinds of wares lodged outside Jerusalem once or twice. But I warned them and said to them, "Why do you lodge outside the wall? If you do so again, I will lay hands on you." From that time on they did not come on the Sabbath. Then I commanded the Levites that they should purify themselves and come and guard the gates, to keep the Sabbath day holy (Nehemiah 13:15-23).

Here the Israelites are getting their Sunday lunch from their local ethnic restaurant. Foreigners are coming to sell their food and goods on the Sabbath. And the Israelites are buying from them, and some are joining their example and getting ahead on their day off. Nehemiah's message? Stop it or I will beat you up!

In all seriousness, Nehemiah sets us a really helpful principle for the Sabbath: no buying or selling. If you think about it, this is an effective way to not rest at the expense of others. If no transactions of any kind are taking place, everyone can stop and rest. I have found that this can also be really healthy for our souls. It teaches our minds to be content for a day. No scrolling Amazon or spending a day at the mall. Sabbath is a day to be content with what we have and to delight in what God has already blessed us with.

The goal of Sabbath is for everyone to be able to have a day of rest. We are to not become a 7-eleven people. We are not to become like Pharaoh driving others into the ground with nonstop work. We are not to rest at the expense of the poor or of those in a lower income bracket. Now, we cannot choose these ways of rest for others or force the Pharaohs of this world to stop oppressing their workers (unless we are called to champion the message of "Let my people go so that they may worship me"), but we can choose to start the change by being obedient ourselves.

Now I must confess that I still have room to grow in this area. When traveling or on vacation, I have bought food from others. I have caused hotel people to be at work. When guests have visited and I did not plan for sufficient leftovers to feed everyone, I have ordered pizza. As a college student, I ate out frequently on my Sabbath. But I am growing in this area. I am intentionally choosing to avoid travel on my Sabbath. I am being more intentional about my day of preparation and making sure there is abundant food available. In closing, again, we have so much freedom in Christ concerning this matter. But the goal set by God is to not rest at the expense of those around us.

The final core ingredients of our Sabbath sundae is that the Sabbath is to the Lord. In most of the Sabbath passages that I have quoted, the phrase "to the Lord" has been used. It is a day holy to the Lord, a Sabbath to the Lord. What does this mean? It means that Sabbath is rest as an act of worship. It is a day to refocus our lives on God. It is a day to worship him. The Jews used the Sabbath as an opportunity for the community to come to the synagogue and hear scripture read. It is a good day for a time of corporate worship and to hear scripture. Sabbath is a day to delight in what God has given us in both family and material blessings. Sabbath is a spiritual practice that allows our souls to rest in God and his goodness. It also means that Sabbath is not just a day for self help, for us to focus on our needs and do whatever we want. Sabbath is ultimately an act of worship and obedience to God.

All In

I believe that these five things are core to the Sabbath: rest from labor and work; quiet, restorative, solemn rest; a consistent day of rest; rest not at the expense of others; and rest as an act of worship to the Lord. If we have these key ingredients I think we have tremendous freedom to flavor the Sabbath how we like or feel called to. I already used the example of food and cooking to display this freedom, but I want to share a few more practices that I have found helpful in my observation of the Sabbath. Take them or leave them as you feel them helpful.

My family has found that starting Sabbath with a feast is the way to go. I used to observe the Sabbath on Sunday from midnight to midnight. Now we observe the Sabbath from sundown on

Saturday to sundown on Sunday. This means that Sabbath usually starts around dinner on Saturday. We prepare a feast of sorts and then enter Sabbath around the table reconnecting as a family and delighting in God's provision of food for us. Then we can rest and talk, maybe play a board game, and just be. Once the Sabbath ends, we then have space on Sunday night after the sun has gone down to prepare for the week ahead.

In connection with this, we almost always light two candles at our Sabbath feast, a candle to remember the Sabbath and a candle to observe the Sabbath. (These are the two commands in Exodus and Deuteronomy: remember and observe). This helps us remember what we are doing and why we are doing it. It is also helpful for guests at our table to see, so that we can explain why we're doing what we're doing without it getting weird. We also always read a short passage of scripture after we light these candles to focus our hearts on God.

Something else I have found helpful is to take a break from most electronics on Sabbath. I still use my Kindle and microwave and such, but I turn off my phone either for all or most of the twenty four hours. I take a break from playing video games on the Sabbath. We take a break from TV and movies unless as a family we feel that a small dose of that would be very restful and restorative and worshipful. We live in a world where screens dominate and demand our attention, and I have found it healing and freeing to my mind, body, and soul to take a break from them for a day each week.

These are just a few practices, but I have found them life-giving. In line with this I must point out that Sabbath is a good time to expose and free us from our idols. Is my phone becoming an idol? Sabbath exposes my dependence on it and then breaks my dependence on it through my regular practice of taking a break from it. Is shopping becoming an idol? Sabbath exposes my need for it and breaks me of that dependence. Am I becoming a workaholic? Sabbath exposes that and trains me in a new way. I must point out that the first months of practicing a Sabbath with these practices were hard. There was much breaking and uprooting of the addictions in my life, things that I loved too much. And that was painful. I say this as a warning, but also as an encouragement that it gets much easier and better over time. And eventually the regular practice of Sabbath caused me to live the other six days differently, with more freedom, energy, and purpose.

In the discussion on rest and Sabbath, I must point out another biblical practice on rest, a cousin to the Sabbath. This is the practice of Sabbatical. My goal in talking about the Sabbath has been to encourage and invite you to begin practicing it. My goal in talking about Sabbatical is to inform you of a different way of living and to maybe pique your interest for the future.

Daniel Bartlett

In connection with the Sabbath in the Law of Moses, there is an additional command of rest: Sabbatical.

> *The Lord spoke to Moses on Mount Sinai, saying, "Speak to the people of Israel and say to them, When you come into the land that I give you, the land shall keep a Sabbath to the Lord. For six years you shall sow your field, and for six years you shall prune your vineyard and gather in its fruits, but in the seventh year there shall be a Sabbath of solemn rest for the land, a Sabbath to the Lord. You shall not sow your field or prune your vineyard. You shall not reap what grows of itself in your harvest, or gather the grapes of your*

undressed vine. It shall be a year of solemn rest for the land. The Sabbath of the land shall provide food for you, for yourself and for your male and female slaves and for your hired worker and the sojourner who lives with you, and for your cattle and for the wild animals that are in your land: all its yield shall be for food...

Therefore you shall do my statutes and keep my rules and perform them, and then you will dwell in the land securely. The land will yield its fruit, and you will eat your fill and dwell in it securely. And if you say, 'What shall we eat in the seventh year, if we may not sow or gather in our crop?' I will command my blessing on you in the sixth year, so that it will produce a crop sufficient for three years. When you sow in the eighth year, you will be eating some of the old crop; you shall eat the old until the ninth year, when its crop arrives" (Leviticus 25:1-7,18-23).

We see here again the rhythm of six and one. Work the land for six years and then in the seventh year let it rest. This is the Sabbatical year. Here God gives the Israelites a sound agricultural principle that farmers still practice today. Ground needs to lie fallow regularly in order to stay fertile. I have agricultural friends who could talk your ear off on all the scientific principles and benefits behind this, but all we will say here is that the land needs rest.

Now, the focus of this command is on the land. But there is a very helpful principle behind this command for the people. And we can say with Paul, "Is it for the oxen that God is concerned? Does he not certainly speak for our sake" (1 Corinthians 9:9-10)?

God gave this command of a Sabbatical to an agricultural society. And in the application of this command, the entire Israelite society took a whole year off from their main vocational work. With a year off from working the land they were free to rest, dream, spend abundant time with family, try something new, invest in a hobby, etc. The Sabbatical year was a year of rest for the land, but it ended up being a year of rest for the people too. This was God's good gift of regular rest to them.

In our modern world, we have a concept of a Sabbatical, but it is isolated to the academic and pastoral worlds. In the modern sense of this idea, professors take a semester off of teaching and instead spend a lot of time researching and writing. This has its origins in the Biblical Sabbatical, but it is not the same. In the pastoral world, it is closer to the Biblical idea. Pastors usually take a few months off from preaching and sometimes go on an extended retreat, but it is limited to the world of ministry.

God's original command for the Sabbatical year gave the entire community a year of rest from vocational work. And this is what I think is God's heart for us as a people. Imagine a world where every seven years you quit your job and took a year off of paid work. What could you do with that year? Invest in a neglected hobby? Reconnect with your family? Reconnect with God? Sleep in for months? Rest? Have your soul be refreshed in God's rest? Seek God's will for what the next six years should look like?

I believe this rest is Biblical and possible for you and me. Now people don't change much over time. And the first thing that comes to most of our minds is what came to the minds of the Israelites. "What shall we eat in the seventh year, if we may not sow or gather in our crop?" God's answer, "I will command my blessing on you in the sixth year, so that it will produce a crop sufficient for three years. When you sow in the eighth year, you will be eating some of the old crop; you shall eat the old until the ninth year, when its crop arrives." In other words, God says that in year six he will provide enough money for year six, the Sabbatical year, and the next year while we get back on our feet.

If anyone still thinks that this is a bit crazy or wouldn't work in your life, may I gently say that that is simply because you do not trust God's ability to provide. I know it is hard to trust and believe, but he is able.

How do I know? This is what God has done for me. My family is currently in month four of our first Sabbatical. Last year God provided for over a year's worth of income in addition to last year's need. We have enough to live on for this year and while I search for a new job when our Sabbatical is over. God is faithful and able to provide.

I know of others and have been mentored by people who regularly take Sabbaticals every seven years. One person in particular is a businessman who has a method of saving a seventh of his income over the six years and then lives on this money during his Sabbatical year. To my knowledge he is currently in his third Sabbatical. I respect this person a lot, and I think this method of saving overflow money over six years instead of waiting until the last year is a sound principle for our non-agricultural society. God promised the Israelites overflow that they would be able to save for the seventh year. In their agricultural society it was necessary for that overflow to occur in the sixth year because food goes bad. In our monetary society, I believe that overflow can occur anytime during the six years, maybe little by little each year or maybe all at once. Either way God promises to provide if we commit ourselves to living this way.

Hopefully these two examples at least put it in your mind that the Sabbatical is financially possible. I have worked in low level fast food and administration jobs for most of my working life, so you do not need to be rich to do this. God is the one who is rich and who richly provides.

If you still have doubts and all this seems fantastical, I would encourage you to start small rather than not starting at all. Try a few weeks or a few months if a year seems too daunting. Schedule a whole summer or half a year off instead. God can be trusted, and he can provide for everything you need in this time of rest.

Now, with this question of finances put to the side. What does a Sabbatical look like in the modern world? In short, it looks like a year or an extended time of rest from our main vocational work. It might also look like us stepping back from other activities that dominate or consume our time, for example, sports or a particular ministry. The Sabbatical year is a time of rest and refreshment. Similar to the Sabbath it is meant to restore us for the next six years of work.

For me this Sabbatical has been one of God's great gifts to me personally. It has been a time of rich blessings after a season of hardship. It has been a time where there has been space for the Lord to refocus my heart and life on him. It has been a time of rest and refreshment after burn out and chronic exhaustion. It has been a time of finding my identity in something other than work. It has been a time to trust the Lord that there will be a place for me once I search again for a job. It has been a time to write, and dream, and learn new skills. It has been a time of joy in the Lord.

I will stop here. I know for a fact that my experience is not an anomaly. Others have experienced these things too, and this idea of Sabbatical is beginning to catch on in our world.

All In

Both Christians and non-Christians alike are catching God's vision for the Sabbatical year and trying to implement it. God has given us such a good gift in his commands to rest. Now you know, and I hope one day you too will get to experience this extended time of rest in Sabbatical.

Rest as an act of worship. A whole day each week set apart to the Lord. A whole year every seven devoted to restoration. Holy gifts given to us by God. This is the Sabbath and the Sabbatical. We live in a restless world, and our hearts cry out for rest and peace. My friend, there is life in God's commands. There are rich blessings, rest, restoration, delight, and so much more found in God's commands to set aside these times of holy rest. We are not bound to observe these things, but

I hope that you now see that we will be blessed if we do.

HOLINESS

"In the year that king Uzziah died I saw the Lord sitting upon a throne, high and lifted up..." -Isaiah 6:1

In this vision the ancient prophet, Isaiah, is transported into the temple in Jerusalem and the temple seems to have come alive. On the normally empty throne, the LORD is sitting, high and lifted up. Like a bride on her wedding day, the train of his robe fills the temple. And the statues of angels

131

and the angels carved on the walls have come alive, are flying around, and are crying out, "Holy, Holy, Holy is the Lord of hosts" (Isaiah 6:3).

It is this phrase that I want us to draw our attention to: "Holy, Holy, Holy is the Lord of hosts." Out of all of God's attributes the angels choose to declare that God is holy? But what does it mean that God is holy? And does it affect us? Well, in short holy means without sin. God is without sin. That is simple enough. But does this affect us? Well, yes. Let me use three analogies to explain this.

First, light. Light is without darkness. By nature of what light is, it chases away (or shall we say destroys) darkness. In the same way God's holiness is like light. Unfortunately for us, that means that when sin comes into direct contact with God's holiness, his holiness destroys it. Simple by nature of what they both are. They cannot coexist.

Another analogy of this is soap and dirt. When soap comes into contact with dirt, it destroys it, simply by nature of what both things are. They cannot coexist.

We see this theological truth in Isaiah's vision. In response to being in God's presence and hearing the angels declare God's holiness, he cries out, "Woe is me! For I am lost; for I am a man of unclean lips, and I dwell in the midst of a people of unclean lips; for my eyes have seen the King, the LORD of hosts" (Isaiah 6:5). In other words, "I'm a dead man. I have sinned. And I have seen the

LORD." When Isaiah came into the presence of the Lord, he realized that he was in big trouble.

Now I promised three analogies and the third is this. I used to work in a used cardboard box warehouse. We would sort, clean, and package massive 50-pound cardboard boxes that major food producers would use to store and transport goods like cereal and noodles and such. And there came a day when *they* came. The age of men was over; the time of the mice had come. The war had begun.

Now, mice in a warehouse dealing with food products is a really bad thing. And they ended up pooping on a lot of the boxes that were meant to hold your morning bowl of cereal. We began a campaign double checking every inch of every box to make sure they were clean before shipping them off to the factories. Some boxes had a speck of poop on them. We threw those away. Some were covered in poop. We threw those away. No matter if the box was covered or if there was a tiny blip of it. It had to go.

I think this is a useful analogy because I have heard it often said, "Oh, I'm not too bad of a person. I've done more good than bad. I think I'll go to heaven when I die." This phrase spawns from a terrible misunderstanding of God's holiness. When we stand before God's throne on the day of judgment, it doesn't matter if we have a speck of sin or are covered in it. We will have to go. Just like darkness in the presence of light or dirt in contact with soap, God's holiness by nature of what it is must destroy and banish us from his presence forever.

Yikes! Like Isaiah we can cry out, "Woe is me! I am lost!"

Yet, that wasn't the end of Isaiah's story. As he cried out, one of the angels approached him with a burning coal from God's altar, touched his lips, and declared, "Your guilt is taken away, and your sin is atoned for" (Isaiah 6:7). Isaiah was clean? He was holy? He could stand before God? Now, this is all highly symbolic, but the truth is Isaiah was made holy by something outside himself. He was made holy by God himself. And now, he could exist in God's presence without being destroyed.

All In

There was hope for Isaiah. Is there hope for us?

You have probably heard it said that by dying on the cross and rising from the dead Jesus takes away our sins if we believe in him. This is true. This is our hope. But I am a curious fellow, and to be honest for a long time that statement made no sense. Why in the world does Jesus dying on the cross take away sin? I don't just like to know what. I like to know why. This has a habit of getting me into trouble, but here I think knowing why is helpful.

It all goes back to creation. God made a perfect world with perfect people who all lived in perfect harmony with God. But the people wanted to be like God. They wanted more. They overstepped their bounds and rebelled against God. This led to sin entering the world. In that brief moment of perfection, God told people that if they disobeyed him they would die. The early Church correspondent, Paul, said it like this, "The wages of sin is death" (Romans 6:23). Sin leads to death. Death is the punishment or consequence for sin.

Okay. Sin leads to death. That tracks with what we know about sin and God's holiness. But how does that lead to Jesus? Well, God is not only holy. He is also love. And out of love he began a plan to restore his creation to perfection.

He chose an ancient family to be his people, his means of saving the world. We know them today as the Jews. To the Jews he gave a law. In this law he revealed how to live holy lives before him. This included laws about what counts as sin, laws about ritual purity, and laws about sacrifice. It is this last bit that is especially relevant to us.

Buried in the early chapters of Leviticus, an ancient text which very few people choose to read, there is a description of an ancient ceremony. It goes like this. The Jews would take a bull or a goat from their herds. It had to be spotless without blemish, a firstborn, and a year old. In other words it had to be as close as possible to perfection. They would take this creature to the temple and lay their hand on its head. This symbolized their sin being transferred onto it. Then the priests would sacrifice the animal. This was known as the sin offering.

This whole ceremony had a very simple idea. Sin deserves death. But God made a way for his people to live before him. They could transfer their sins onto another "perfect," "sinless" creature, and it could die in their place. It took their sin and punishment for them, and they could live as a holy people before God.

In principle, this is the system that God set up for a sinful people to be able to exist in his presence. Like Isaiah, their sin could be taken away. The only problem was that these animals weren't truly perfect. They represented perfection, but they were not it. As the writer of the letter known as Hebrews says, "It is impossible for the blood of bulls and goats to take away sins" (Hebrews 10:4). This snag in the system meant that the Jews had to offer sacrifice after sacrifice, year after year.

And this is where we get to Jesus and why his death on the cross "works." God himself became a man. He taught us how to live before him. He lived a perfect, sinless life. And then the priests devised his death. He died on the cross as the true, perfect, sinless sacrifice. And now, just like how the Jews put their hands on the animals to transfer their sin onto them, whoever believes in Jesus has their sin transferred onto him as the sacrifice that dies in their place. As the iconic verse says, "For God so loved the world that he gave his only Son, that whoever believes in him should not perish but have eternal life" (John 3:16).

So, like Isaiah, there is hope for us. God has made a way for us to live in his holy presence. We need not be destroyed. We can be clothed in Christ's righteousness and be sinless before God.

If you are a Christian and you've read this far, you've probably been like, "Yeah, yeah, yeah. I know most of this stuff." But I say it all because it is essential to understand the foundation before we move on. Because, if you are a Christian, I think it is important for us to then understand our identity as saints. And I believe in the Church today some Christians believe that they are still sinners when actually they are not.

I want to challenge you with some verses. "No one who abides in him keeps on sinning; no one who keeps on sinning has either seen him or known him" (1 John 3:6). "No one born of God makes a practice of sinning, for God's seed abides in him; and he cannot keep sinning, because he has been born of God" (1 John 3:9). "How can we who died to sin still live in it?" (Romans 6:2). "We know that our old self was crucified with him in order that the body of sin might be brought to nothing, so that we would no longer be enslaved to sin" (Romans 6:6). "Let not sin therefore reign in your mortal body, to make you obey its passions" (Romans 6:12). "For no good tree bears bad fruit, nor again does a bad tree bear good fruit" (Luke 6:43).

This is just a sample of the teachings of Jesus and his disciples. And this is my point: once a person becomes a Christian, their nature fundamentally changes. We go from being a "bad tree" to a "good tree." Our old sin nature dies, and we are born again into a new life of holiness. Because of Jesus, our very nature and identity changes. We go from sinners who do good once in a while to saints who mess up once in a while. We are clothed in Christ's righteousness and holiness and are called into a new way of living and of being. We are called to be holy.

"You shall be holy, for I am holy" -God (1 Peter 1:16).

I have heard it often said by my brothers and sisters, "Oh, I'm a sinner in need of grace." "We're still sinners." "I'm a sinner through and through, but thanks be to God for his mercy." These phrases sound very pious and spiritual. But these phrases spring from a misunderstanding of the work that Jesus has done to us and in us.

Don't get me wrong. We were sinners. We were dead in our trespasses and sins. We were without hope and gone. But God in his great mercy made us alive. Our status has changed. We are saints. To say we're still sinners is to say that we are still dead after Christ has made us alive. It is to minimize the work of Christ in our lives.

Let me give one very clear example of my point. In the New Testament letters Christians are never addressed as sinners. Never. Just read the first paragraph of half the letters. "To the saints in Colossae." "To the saints in Philippi." "To the saints in Ephesus." Even in Corinth where the church had some major sin issues going on, Paul addresses them as those who are called to be saints. In Greek, saints means holy ones. Once someone is made holy by Jesus' sacrifice, their identity changes from a sinner to a holy one.

Why does this matter? It matters because we live into our identity. Now, some of this has to do with semantics. Even Paul, far along in his Christian walk, confessed that he wasn't yet perfect. He still messed up once in a while and sinned. Technically, one could say that if we sin we are sinners. But this really isn't how we use the English language. What in the world do I mean? Well, suppose I walked up to you and said, "I am a basketball player." Now, suppose that I'm super short and not athletic at all. Furthermore, suppose that you knew that I've only played basketball once in my life and it was six years ago. What would you say? I don't think you'd agree with my statement. A basketball player is someone who plays and practices basketball regularly. They are someone who knows the game intimately. Technically, I did play basketball, once. So technically, I am a basketball player. But no real basketball player would ever accept me as one of their own. When we make *I am* statements in English, we're making identity statements. So when we say that we are sinners, we are communicating that our identity is bound to sin. Sin is a regular part of our life. Sin for a sinner is natural. It's not a big deal. It's to be expected. On the other hand, sin for a saint is unnatural. It's an odd occurrence. It's responded to in grief and repentance and then God's grace instead of apathy and future condemnation. It's all a question of our identity in Jesus and what we are living into.

My one and single point is this: Christians are called to be holy. God is holy. In Christ's death and sacrifice, we have been made holy. And now we are called to live in light of our new status before God. To be holy as he is holy. To be perfect as he is perfect. To strive to live a new sinless life before him. How do we do this? We walk in step with the *Holy* Spirit who is within us. We rely on his power. We keep ourselves unstained from the world. "Present your bodies as a living sacrifice, holy and acceptable to God, which is your spiritual worship. Do not be conformed to this world, but be transformed by the renewal of your mind" (Romans 12:1-2). This is our call as Christians. Our identity is no longer as sinners. Sinning should be an odd occurrence for us. No one born of God makes a habit of sinning. We are saints. And saints live holy lives.

Let us say with Paul, "Not that I have already obtained this or am already perfect, but I press on to make it my own, because Christ Jesus has made me his own" (Philippians 3:12). For "His divine power has granted to us all things that pertain to life and godliness, through the knowledge of him who called us to his own glory and excellence" (2 Peter 1:3).

As Christians we need to cast away the narrative and the lie of being stuck in sin, and we need to find our identity in who God says we are rather than in our failures. If we still find our identity as sinners and live accordingly, we make little of the work that Jesus has done in our lives. Like Isaiah after the angel declared, "Your guilt is taken away, and your sin atoned for," let us strive to live holy lives in the service of God.

Eternal Impact

How can I have an impact on this world? What is my purpose? What is worth pursuing? Does my life matter to anyone? When I look around at my generation, these are some of the most common questions I see people struggling with. It has been my experience growing up that many of my peers and I have been told that we can be anything we want to be. We can do anything we want to do. You want to be a rocket scientist? Go for it! You want to be a mega-church worship pastor? Why not? My generation has been told that they can change the world.

This encouragement is all well-intentioned and in some ways true. In a globalizing world, my generation does have an enormous amount of opportunity unseen in many other generations. But this encouragement is also burdensome. We don't only feel free to change the world; we feel obligated to change it.

For a time, I worked as a recruiter at a local university, and I would often talk to young people about what they wanted to study in college. Frequently, I would talk to high schoolers wanting to study nursing. Our conversations often went something like this: "So you want to study nursing. That's great! Do you enjoy science?"

"No. I actually hate science, especially biology."

"Why do you want to study nursing then?"

"I want to help people."

(For those of you who don't know, nursing has a fair amount to do with science, especially biology).

I found that most people entering college were wanting to study things that they thought would help them help others and make a difference in the world, something that would give their life meaning. At the Christian college where I went to school, our professors told us that we would become the leading scientists, scholars, doctors, missionaries, engineers, communicators, and the like. Our motto was *For Christ and His*

Kingdom, and we were being trained to make an eternal impact in the world. Because of this, it came as quite a shock to many of us once we graduated and the world didn't seem to realize that we were ready to change it. Many of us were surprised to find ourselves working at fast food restaurants and ice-cream shops or working as low-level telemarketers and office assistants; we were surprised to find ourselves being turned down for our dream teaching positions or being turned away from mission agencies. We found ourselves struggling to pay our most basic bills and rent. And that person who we fell in love with in college and who was going to be the second half of our power couple—well, it turns out marriage is a little bit more complicated than that.

All In

Many, in my experience, have experienced this slap in the face when the reality of life sinks in. Instead of going overseas, I'm going to the grocery store. Instead of changing my community, I'm changing diapers. Instead of working in a skyscraper, I'm working in the basement. And when this reality sinks in, all the questions start to come. Does my life matter to anyone? What is my purpose? What is worth pursuing? How will I ever make an impact on the world?

I have written this to answer these questions, because you can change this world. And not only can you change this world, but you can impact this world for all eternity. Let me tell you a story, so you know where we are headed.

Daniel Bartlett

It was Friday evening, and a group of us college kids were sitting in a small conference room eating food from Saga, our cafeteria. Our group was officially known as the Chicago Evangelism Team, and we were grabbing dinner together before we hopped on a train and took the short trip into downtown Chicago to talk with people on the streets. While we ate, we were listening to our fearless leader and one of my best friends, Jonathan Vines, give a short devotional. And something he said that night stuck in my brain like molasses. In one short sentence, Jonathan summed up what the Lord had been teaching me for years, and I realized that he had just told us the key to making an eternal impact on the world. "The greatest gift that we can ever give this world is our intimacy with Christ."

The key to making an eternal impact in this world is our intimacy with Christ. What in the world does that mean? Now, before you write this phrase off as entirely unhelpful, let me give you an example of what I am talking about. Let's dive into the reason why angels shine.

Imagine floating in space looking down on the earth, and as you stare down at the big blue and green marble, you begin to soar downward. As you get soaked in the dew of a cloud, you see that you are above a desert area of the Middle East, and it looks like there is a giant Rubik's Cube beneath you. As you look closer, you figure that it can't be a Rubik's Cube because there are twelve blocks instead of nine. Then as you begin to worry about how you're going to stop, you realize that the twelve blocks are actually organized hordes of tents and people. You've traveled back to a time when ancient Israel was wandering in the desert. And if you were to stay a while, you would encounter a curious phenomenon that is recorded in the ancient manuscripts of Exodus 34:34-35.

This phenomenon first occurred when Moses met with God on a mountain. After God had given Moses the Ten Commandments and Moses had moseyed back down the mountain to the encampment of the Israelites, his face shone. And not like a bride on her wedding day, his face was literally glowing. Well, this scares the Israelites to death, so Moses starts wearing a veil to cover his face. And this isn't a one-time occurrence. Moses has this special tent outside the camp where God comes in the form of a cloud and regularly talks with Moses face to face. And whenever Moses leaves, his face is glowing. But why?

To find this out let's travel a couple miles north and a couple hundred years into the future to a silent night. It might even be described as a holy night. And what's so special about this silent night? Well, it's special because it actually isn't too silent. There's lots of screaming, singing, and door-to-door evangelism going on tonight. We've traveled to the overcrowded town of Bethlehem, and tonight, Christ the savior is born.

But, let's focus in on one event of this night: the shepherds watching over their flock at night.

They're just normal shepherd guys doing their normal shepherd stuff. Suddenly, an angel shows up and lights the place up like a torch. Specifically, Luke 2:9 says, "The glory of the Lord shone around them." Well, these shepherds are terrified, but the angel tells them about Jesus being born and then, with some back-up singers, launches into a song that would make any musical director proud. But let's focus on what we've come to this night to see. An angel shows up, and he glows. Specifically, he shines with the glory of God. Sounds kind of like Moses.

Now before we come to a conclusion about what in the world is happening here, let's go to one more place just a couple miles to the north and a couple years into the future.

All In

This time we've come to the city of Jerusalem. Jesus has already ascended into heaven, and the Church has begun to take off. On this specific day, a man stands before the Jewish leaders giving a bold speech. This guy has some mad street preaching skills, and nobody has been able to beat him in a biblical argument about Jesus. So his opponents, unaware of the pithy saying, "If you can't beat them, join them." drag Stephen to court and give some false testimony about him to try to destroy him. But a curious thing happens. While Stephen gives his defense, his face begins to shine like an angel. And as he finishes his rather offensive speech, Acts 7:55 says, "He, full of the Holy Spirit, gazed into heaven and saw the glory of God, and Jesus standing at the right hand of God." Again, we find a situation where a person's face shines.

So what is going on with these three stories? Why do Moses, the angel, and Stephen all shine? The key to understanding this is found in the phrase, "The glory of God." Stephen was full of the Holy Spirit. Moses spent time with God in the tent of meeting. The angel practically lived in God's presence. Each of these three people/beings spent time in God's presence and came away reflecting God's glory. Like a sponge, each absorbed God's glory while in his presence, and once they left, it oozed out of their appearance. This reflection of God terrified the Israelites, brought the shepherds to their knees, and frightened the Jewish council. The point I am trying to make here is that when one spends time in God's presence, it shows in a powerful way. That person begins to reflect God himself to others. In other words, intimacy with God leads to personal transformation which leads to impacting others.

In case these examples do not explain my point well enough, let me give one analogy to make this all clear. The heavens declare the glory of God, and they can give us a helpful picture of how truly knowing Christ can impact the world. Let us take the earth, sun, and moon and see how they apply to us.

During the day, the sun gives the earth light, a lot of light. But as the earth turns around, part of it begins to face away from the sun, and we enter into the world of night. The moon circles the earth, and depending on its angle might give some light as well. The moon has a reflective surface, and the better view of the sun that it has, the more light it reflects onto the earth. If the earth gets in between its view of the sun, it stops shining. Of course, you already knew all of this! You learned it in elementary school. So what's my point?

Jesus says in John 9, "I am the light of the world." and "Night is coming." While Jesus walked on the earth, he was the light of the world like the sun in daytime. When he left, night came. Now, the earth is shrouded in darkness. But Jesus says of his people, "You are the light of the world." Like the moon shining in the night we are to shine Christ's light into the dark world. Like the moon we have been taken out of the world. Peter says that we are strangers and aliens on the earth. We, through the Holy Spirit, also have a unique perspective of Jesus and a relationship with him that the world cannot have. Like the moon we see Christ directly while the dark world cannot. I hope you see my point in all of this, for the moon, while very different from the world, does not have any light of its own. It can only reflect the sun's light. The fuller its view of the sun, the brighter it shines. If it lets the world get in between its view of the sun, it doesn't shine. In the same way, as we stare into the face of Christ and live in close relationship with him, we will naturally reflect Christ to others. But if we let the world get in between us and Jesus, then we will be like the crescent moon and only shine a little. If we spend no time with Christ, the world won't even be able to tell us apart from its own black sky. I fear in this situation the believer has quenched the Spirit. I think in this analogy the impact is clear. If we try to be witnesses for Christ apart from intimacy with him, we will fail. If we have a close relationship with God, it will naturally show to the world even if we make no other efforts to "change the world." Therefore intimacy with Christ is the greatest gift we can give this world. Knowing Christ and spending time with him is the prerequisite for any real ministry and for living an impactful life. Effort apart from intimacy with Christ is in vain.

Before I go on, let me be clear. When I'm talking about making a difference in the world, I'm not talking about helping Carl across his yard, rescuing those stray kittens, or even paying for someone else's groceries. You do not need to believe in God to do these things. While I worked at Chick-fil-A, we had a system we called IAKs, or intentional acts of kindness. Every employee was given $10 to give away during their shift. My coworkers who knew nothing of God were able to make a person's day with this gift just as well as me. While Christians should be generous, kind, giving people, and often the Holy Spirit does command us to be pioneers in these daily acts of kindness, some of the kindest people I know are not Christians. Athletes, celebrities, and billionaires can do good things and change people's lives without knowing God. This kind of impact is not what I am talking about. I am talking about what Jesus said when he told his disciples that they would do greater things than him, doing things that are impossible without the Spirit of God. If you are wondering what that looks like, we will look at the lives of Spirit-filled Christians in a later section. But it is enough to say here that we are talking about a Jesus-sized impact on the world.

Now, if there is a formula for intimacy for Christ, I don't pretend to know it. And what I mean by *formula* is the temptation in American society to make everything into a three-step process. Go to college, volunteer in some good clubs, and get some valuable work experience, and you will be able to get a good job. Do this and that and this, and this will happen. I have been tempted in the past with this formula approach to my relationship with God. I have often thought that if I spend an hour a day reading my Bible and in prayer, if I fast from excessive entertainment such as more than two or three hours of television and video games a week, and if I am an active member of a local church, then I will be close with God. But the more I have tried this and other such formulas (and tried to oppress them on others) the more I realize that life and relationships are more complicated than this. I suspect that there is no one formula for intimacy with Christ.

So if intimacy is the agent of real eternal impact on the world, how do we have intimacy with the Lord? Well, while there is no three-step formula for this relationship, God has made it clear in scripture for how this is possible, and I encourage you to go search in scripture for yourself to find out what Jesus says. But I will harp on two points here that are near and dear to my heart: the cost of discipleship and the power of the Holy Spirit.

When I began following Christ eight years ago, he called me to give up everything for him. Video games, movies, TV, my love life, my friends, social media, fictional books, everything that filled my time and my heart. The Holy Spirit's constant refrain was, "Me or Xbox?" "Me or TV?" "Me or such-and-such a thing?" God called me to give up everything to follow him. And it was then that I began to learn that God wants nothing less than all that we are. For two years I abstained from all that the Lord called me away from. For two years as a teenager I didn't watch a movie; I didn't play a video game. The Lord was always faithful and blessed me generously so that my sacrifices were never really sacrifices. I gained far more than I gave up. After a time in the wilderness with him, he gave me a new church community to replace my video game community. He gave me ministries to be involved in to fill my time and to give me purpose. He gave me missionary biographies for entertainment and inspiration. He gave me his own dear presence and joy worthy of any sacrifice. But it was here that I learned it is all or nothing with God. Jesus says as much in the Gospels. "Any one of you who does not renounce all that he has cannot be my disciple" (Luke 14:33). "If anyone would come after me, let him deny himself and take up his cross daily and follow me. For whoever would save his life will lose it, but whoever loses his life for my sake will save it" (Matthew 16:24-25). I learned this lesson in those years, but the Lord has had to ingrain it in me through much trial and error. There is so much temptation in the idea of Christ plus something: Christ and a guilty pleasure here and there; Christ and a questionable movie once in a while; Christ and a little bit of the world; I am all yours Christ, but I need just a bit of side action when I'm really stressed or tired. God you can have all of me as long as you stay away from my sports or video games! God has taught me that this is unacceptable to him. He is worthy of our all, and he will not settle for less. Whenever I have fallen into the temptations of Christ and some part of the world (and believe me this has happened many times in the past few years), God will remove his joy, peace, and presence from me. He does this for my good, to draw me back into his best for me. And he is patient; for he has to do it often. But his presence (and I'm talking about his presence in real power and joy) is better than life.

I can hear many readers' objections at this point, "Daniel, you are just being an extremist in your faith! God doesn't want me to give up all that. God delights giving his children things to enjoy. I won't give up all that." Well, maybe I am an extremist, but if you read the Gospels, you will find that Jesus is a bit of an extremist too. And he demands his followers to be extremists for him.

And on that second note, God does give his children very good gifts to enjoy! God created this earth and the things in it to be very good. He made us in his image to be creative people and to delight in the good things that we can create. We were made to live embodied lives that delight in God and his creation. A helpful check is to ask yourself whether you are delighting in what God has given you or what you have taken for yourself and to ask whether Christ is everything to you and everything else is just some tasty icing on top or whether your life consists of Christ and... .

The point in all of this is that I have found that to have intimacy with God is an all or nothing affair. There is a cost to following Jesus, and you must either pay it or walk away. God will not settle for anything less than your everything. In my experience, there can be no true intimacy with him until you can honestly say like Paul, "I count everything as loss because of the surpassing worth of knowing Christ Jesus my Lord. For his sake I have suffered the loss of all things and count them as rubbish, in order that I may gain Christ" (Philippians 3:8).

I have used examples of things like video games, fictional books, and movies because that is what is relevant to my life. Each of us will have different things that hold power over our lives and things we must surrender to Jesus. It could be relationships, ice-cream, knitting magazines, the opera, the Office, or anything else. There are other contributing factors to our intimacy with the Lord.

I can't name them all here, and I do not presume to know them all. One most recent thing for me was my holding onto my need to make a name for myself in the world and get a certain degree. The Lord was heavy with me while I hung tightly to my rebellion, but as soon as I surrendered, he poured out such rich blessings on me. I urge you to find out what God says for himself in his Word about knowing him. He is worth it, and if you desire to impact the world, the cost is necessary. Now, I must also talk about the role of the Holy Spirit for it gives us a very practical outlook on how to live fully for Christ.

Imagine a war zone, a field with two large hills on each side with buildings in between. Now picture two armies battling against each other.

All In

Depending on what era you've pictured, maybe there are catapults, or cannons, or mortars on the hills firing upon the opposite armies, and maybe the soldiers are fighting each other in the valley with swords, or muskets, or machine guns. Now I want you to picture yourself. You are a wealthy farmer, and these two armies are fighting over your land. Whoever wins will rule over you and your land. Now, you might be able to give someone a nasty jab with your pokey pitchfork, but you aren't a soldier and don't have a major part in the fighting. What can you do but sit by and watch? These two armies fight on and on with neither gaining any ground, and it seems like this war will never end. But soon each army runs out of food supplies. You, as a wealthy farmer, have massive stores of food and the ability to feed the two armies. Yet, what should you do? One of the armies promises fun and pleasure once it wins the battle and rules over you. But when you look around at the other lands that this army rules over, all you see is death and destruction. Will this happen to your land too? The other army seems rather dull and boring, and they ask a lot of you. But when you look at the lands that this army rules over, you see life and adventure. Well, the rule of both armies seems to have some appeal, so you decide to feed both a fairly steady diet. Some days the promise of pleasure and fun seem more exciting, so you send over extra food to the one army. Other days, the life that the other army promises seems worth the cost, and you send over more food to that army to bolster their chances of winning the battle with well-fed soldiers. The fighting continues until you eventually starve out one army and feed the other to victory. These two armies are commonly referred to as the flesh and the Spirit.

This is a real battle, one that is being fought inside you at this very moment. If you are a Christian, then you have the Holy Spirit dwelling within you wanting to reign over your life. You also have your sinful flesh that promises great things but never really delivers. You are also like the farmer in our story. You control the food supply. How many hours a day do you spend feeding the desires of your flesh, watching that TV show, playing that video game, spending time with those friends who are a bad influence on you, or doing whatever worldly investment is tempting to you? And how many hours a day do you spend feeding the Spirit, spending time with other Christians, serving others, reading your Bible, praying, fasting, worshiping, giving thanks, and the like? Which army is winning in your life?

Let me give a very tangible example of what this looks like in real life. Have you ever gone to church camp, or sent your kids to church camp, or maybe gone to a Christian conference or on a mission trip? During camp kids are often forced to leave their phones and other tech at home, and day after day at these week-long camps there are Bible studies, worship sessions, Christian community, clean fun, and constant godly preaching and council. Kids are encouraged to spend time in the Word of God and prayer, and they have constant Christian community with others. There are also usually preplanned, meaningful activities designed to feed the Spirit. Often at these camps these kids feel connected to others, they give their lives to Christ, and they have other life transforming experiences where God becomes everything to them. They gain an overwhelming passion to pursue Christ. But then they go home and daily life kicks in, and everything goes back to normal. Have you ever experienced this or seen this happen? I have, many times. But why? Why does this happen?

Well, let's go back to our analogy of the battle between the flesh and the Spirit. When having these camp-like experiences, the Spirit gets an enormous food boost. All the Bible study, worship, prayer, and good community feed the Spirit within us. At the same time the usual things that we use to feed our flesh get cut off, and the flesh becomes starved. This situation, with the Spirit getting super buff and the flesh becoming ragged and starved, lets the Spirit get victory over the battlefield and reign over your life with the promised transformation that follows. But once camp is over and daily life resumes, we start feeding the flesh again and slowly begin to starve out the victorious Spirit. The flesh is able to lead a rebellion and start gaining ground again.

I hope this example makes clear this battle between the flesh and the Spirit. Paul talks about this battle in Galatians 5:16-17 when he says, "Walk by the Spirit, and you will not gratify the desires of the flesh. For the desires of the flesh are against the Spirit, and the desires of the Spirit are against the flesh, for these are opposed to each other." Peter also talks about this in 1 Peter 2:11: "I urge you as sojourners and exiles to abstain from the passions of the flesh, which wage war against your soul." This battle happens throughout our lives with the Spirit getting regular boosts, like when someone first gives their life to Christ or attends a camp or a conference and then the temptations of the flesh fighting back with the pleasures that are so hard to give up. There is a constant battle between the flesh and the Spirit within us.

Daniel Bartlett

As we go on, I do want to take a few steps down a rabbit trail that I think is important to this point. During my experience at churches and in college, there was a lot of talk and focus put on this thing called revival. I myself was a part of a movement of students on my campus praying for revival to fall upon our school. My church spent a whole season where we prayed for and studied revival. We sometimes even schedule weekends for things we call revivals. But I have come to the conclusion that revival should not be a regular part of a Christian's experience. Now, before you burn me at the stake as a heretic, let me explain what I mean.

It was pointed out to me by a friend that there is a difference between what we call revival

184

and spiritual awakening, although we often get the two confused. Spiritual awakening happens when someone comes to Christ, gets saved, invites Jesus into their hearts, is born again, or whatever you like to call it. Their dead spirit is made alive by Jesus' sacrifice, and the Holy Spirit comes to dwell in them. Revival is what we have been talking about. Revival is when suddenly the Spirit gets an unexplainable divine boost and wipes out the flesh after a period of time when the army of the flesh had taken over the battle ground and had been reigning supreme over the Spirit in someone's life. We usually associate this type of revival with repentance and a renewal of a zealous passion for God.

Daniel Bartlett

I mentioned that during my college years, a group of us students spent much time praying for this on our campus. Well, we saw it happen. During my sophomore year, about a hundred people experienced this radical type of revival. Our weekly prayer and worship meeting that normally lasted an hour or so naturally began lasting four to five hours into the early hours of the morning. Evangelism became a priority for many. It was common to see a group of students stopped on the sidewalk praying with someone. Confession became commonplace. Students began gathering in mass before our chapel service and all-school communion to pray over every seat. People were on fire for Jesus. But after a while, this fire began to die out. The pressure of exams and homework and the many other demands and distractions of life began to feed the flesh back up to strength, and everything started to go back to normal.

Revival shouldn't be a part of a Christian's life because we shouldn't ever need it. The fact that we do so often need it is a testament to our Christian commitment and character. Paul's argument in Romans 6 goes along this line. We shouldn't be enslaved to sin or the flesh any longer, because Jesus' death has made a way for us to live and have victory in the Spirit. God has given us everything we need to live a godly life. Jesus has won the battle, and he invites us into that victory. If the flesh reigns in our bodies, it is because we are choosing for it to have control over us. We are feeding it.

We should also not rely on revival because it can lead to a never-ending cycle. It is not sustainable. Being so focused on the idea of revival can lead to the Spirit taking charge of our life only for us to starve it again by feeding the flesh. And then once the flesh is ruling over us, we begin to pray for revival again. We become like the Israelites in the time of the judges. If revival does not lead to habits of Spirit dominance, then that camp-like revival does me little long-term good. For does it not dishonor God if we share in his Spirit, walk away from him, and then try to return over and over again. It is natural for the Christian to live in a constant state of the Spirit ruling in their life.

All In

"Well, this is all well and good in theory, but you can't actually expect me to not feed the flesh at all. It's impossible!" If this is what you are thinking right now, I've written the next section just for you.

We have now gotten to the point where we must talk about temptation. If there is a battle between the flesh and the Spirit in my life, if it is possible to live in a state where the Holy Spirit constantly reigns supreme over the flesh, and if my intimacy with Christ depends on this, then we must figure out how to daily feed the Spirit and resist the temptations to feed the flesh.

First, to those who think this state is impossible, let me direct you to what Paul says in 1 Corinthians 10:13: "No temptation has overtaken you that is not common to man. God is faithful, and he will not let you be tempted beyond your ability, but with the temptation he will also provide the way of escape, that you may be able to endure it." Scripture clearly says that we will not experience any temptation that we do not have the ability to endure. This means that every temptation that the flesh throws at us to get us to feed it can be resisted. And if we have the choice to not feed it, then it means that whenever we do feed it, it is because we chose to. We gave into the temptation.

Temptation, oh what a horrible thing! Irresistible, but so deadly. I think this is the view of many Christians, and it has been my own view for quite a while as well. We view temptation as something that is all bad. So I was quite shocked when I came across this verse in the Bible: "Consider it all joy, my brothers, when you face temptations of various kinds" (James 1:2). It took a while to sink in. Temptation is to be a joy? Why? Well, this scripture goes on: "For you know that the testing of your faith produces steadfastness. And let steadfastness have its full effect, that you may be perfect and complete, lacking in nothing" (James 1:3-4). Interesting. James is saying that temptation is the doorway to spiritual maturity. He re-emphasizes this point later in the passage. "Blessed is the man who remains steadfast under temptation, for when he has stood the test he will receive the crown of life" (James 1:12). Temptation provides the opportunity for us to resist it. Temptation tests our faith and resolve, and when we do resist it, our faith is proved genuine, we gain endurance, and we grow as Christians to eventual reward. James is saying that when temptation comes our way we shouldn't just sweep it under the rug, but rather inwardly rejoice. We have a chance to prove our devotion for Christ and to grow as Christians! What a joy!

After seeing this in James, I began to see the joy of temptation throughout Scripture. We of course are supposed to, as Hebrews says, "consider Jesus" and look to him as our example. And when we do, we see Jesus willingly going into the wilderness to be tempted by the devil for forty days. Jesus endures, gains victory over the devil and his flesh, proves himself faithful, and prepares himself for his ministry as the Messiah. As Hebrews says, "For because he himself has suffered when tempted, he is able to help those who are being tempted" (Hebrews 2:18).

I say all this to change the outlook of those naysayers who think it is impossible for them to resist the flesh and have intimacy with the Spirit. We are to consider resisting the temptations of the flesh a joy! It will make you stronger! It will prove your devotion to Christ and make you into a mature Christian. Christ is by your side to help you, and as long as his promises are true, he will give you the power to overcome. It is possible for you to live a Spirit-filled life. It is possible for you to have intimacy with Christ and to impact the world for him.

Even after all this I think the enemy may be speaking this lie into your heart, for he has often spoken this to me, and he likes to reuse the same tricks against us. "But if you give up this or that, your life will be miserable. What will you do after a long day of work if you give up that particular TV show? Or what will your friends think if you give up this or that? How will you relax? How will you enjoy life? Your life will be ruined!" Let us respond to him, "So be it! Let my life be ruined for Christ! I will give up all for him!" Do not let the enemy deceive you. There may be a bit of truth in his lie, but listen to the words of Jesus. "Whoever wants to be my disciple must deny themselves and take up their cross and follow me. For whoever wants to save their life will lose it, but whoever loses their life for me will find it" (Matthew 16:24-25). There is a paradox here. If we listen to the devil and try to hold on to our lives, we will actually lose everything. If we willingly lose our lives for Jesus, we will find the life that we have been searching for. Let me give one analogy to this point that one of my Greek professors once told me. "The things of this world are like a receding tide. If we cling onto them, we will be swept away with them." We must either choose the world or Jesus. We cannot have both. Let us resist temptation and follow Christ!

Now, before we go on and look at some examples of Christians who have done what we have been talking about, I do need to make a brief note. If you know your Bible or look up the verses I have been quoting, you might say, "Wait a second, Daniel! Those verses in James say consider it joy when you experience trials of various kinds, not temptations! You're twisting the Scriptures!" Well, before you declare with Judah, "Bring him out, and let him be burned," let me explain myself.

Bear with me a moment while I put my academic hat on. The word in James that most Bible translations translate as trials is the Greek word *peirasmos*. Now, this can mean several different things depending on the context: tests, trials, or temptations. An English example of this kind of thing is the word *duck*. Duck can mean two very different things. If we are walking around a farm and I point at a bird and say "duck," I am clearly pointing out to you that I have spotted the animal called duck, and I am trying to draw your attention to it. If we are in the middle of a battlefield and I say "duck," I am clearly trying to tell you to drop to the ground because if you don't you'll probably die. In these examples the word *duck* signals two very different meanings, but context helps clarify them for us. But let us imagine a circumstance where context is less helpful. Suppose I walk into the kitchen and say, "Who cut the cheese?!" This could mean two very different things. But which do I mean? Let us further suppose that Patrick and Emily are both in the kitchen with me. Patrick has just let a silent one rip, and a block of mutilated cheese that we were supposed to have for dinner sits on the counter next to Emily. Again, how can Emily and

Patrick know what I mean when I say, "Who cut the cheese?!" Am I pointing out Emily's bad cheese cutting job or shaming Patrick for his gas? Well, there is a theory of linguistic communication called Relevance Theory, and I will summarize it by saying that we assume what people say will be relevant. Emily probably thinks that I am criticizing her cheese cutting skills, and Patrick is probably blushing embarrassingly because he thinks that I am pointing out his fart, because these things are what are most relevant to Emily and Patrick at this moment. But what do I really mean? Well, there is no way to know for sure unless I continue and clarify my meaning by maybe saying something like, "We were supposed to eat that for dinner!" Or, "That smells so bad!" In that case Emily and Patrick would know what I meant.

James does this same thing. He opens his letter by saying, "Who cut the cheese?!" Or in this case, "Count peirasmos all joy!" What does he mean: temptations, trials, or tests? Well, Greek readers are going to apply Relevance Theory and read it in context of what is most relevant. Am I suffering persecution? I'll probably read it as trials. Am I struggling with temptation? I'll probably read it as that. It could mean either. Some scholars will even wonder if there is even a difference between trials and temptations. I think there is. In English, trials indicate suffering, like walking on hot coals. Temptations indicate something desirable that leads to destruction of some kind.

So is James saying, "You're going to suffer, but you should be happy about it." Or is he talking about temptation?

Our English translations of the Bible are very good, but I think this is one instance where they got it wrong. Why? Because in verse 13 he clarifies what he has been saying in verses 1 and 12. He uses the word *peirazo* which is related to *peirasmos* except that in this context it is pretty clear that it means temptation not trial. Just like when I said, "It smells bad," to clarify what I meant by cutting the cheese, James clarifies that he was talking about temptation when using *peirasmos*. Now rejoicing under trial is still biblical. Other passages such as Romans 5 or 1

Peter say as much. But I think James is saying something different here.

Now that we got that slight issue of heresy out of the way and have an argument that any temptation can be resisted and that living a Spirit-filled life is possible, let's look at people who have lived out what we have been talking about, people who have resisted the temptations of the flesh and lived Spirit-filled impactful lives of intimacy with Christ.

Let us first look at the examples of two extraordinary men who lived lives of Spirit-filled intimacy with Christ and who Jesus used for his kingdom in great ways: George Muller and Hudson Taylor.

These two men were contemporaries of each other and even knew each other. They both lived and worked in the 1800s. George Muller was a Prussian who lived and worked in England most of his adult life. He was a local pastor, a father, and a husband. But he is most famous because of a very curious thing. When he prayed, his prayers were always answered. And not with the modern idea of "God always answers, sometimes it's just a *no*." For George, whatever he prayed for actually happened. He took Jesus' promises about prayer in John 14-17 and put them to the test. And he found God faithful. A great ambition of his life was to show others that prayer matters. When God began to call him to take care of the orphans in Bristol, he obeyed, starting first a breakfast club and then later an orphanage for the poor. (This was a time when orphanages were only for the children of the rich and when poorhouses were common. Think of *Oliver Twist* and Charles Dickens' other writings.) George Muller had no support for his orphanage but trusted entirely on God to supply everything. It was an orphanage run completely on God's provision through prayer. Over his lifetime George helped raise over ten thousand orphans, and even with asking no one for support besides God, nearly one and a half million pounds passed through George Muller's hands to support orphans and other ministries of the day. That is the equivalent of two-hundred, fifty-nine million US dollars in 2022 (according to my internet search). He once was running late for a meeting in Canada and prayed that the fog delaying their ship would lift, and it actually did, immediately. Why did God listen to him? Well, it's reported that George found it necessary to spend up to two or three hours each morning with the Lord before going about his day. He spent his life in the presence of God, and that led to him having an eternal impact on the world. Here is a man who knew God!

Next we turn to his friend, Hudson Taylor. Hudson was an Englishman who lived most of his life as a missionary doctor in China. Hudson gave up the chance for a comfortable life as a doctor in England. He had to let go of the woman he loved and all of life's comforts. And by the time he was twenty-one, he was pioneering the gospel into inland China. Hudson Taylor pioneered a new way of doing missions for that time (living incarnationally with the local people), and throughout his life he led others to live by faith, give up all for Christ, and bring the gospel into the heart of China. He founded China Inland Mission, which thrived to become probably one of the most influential mission organizations to date for the gospel of Jesus Christ. He was a main influence in the evangelization of China. And what was his secret? Daily, hourly fellowship with God through prayer and feeding upon God's Word. God was first in his life, not his mission, not the people of China, not the need, nor anything else. His delight, focus, and constant trust was on God.

As another example, let's look at Lillian Trasher. Lillian was an artist from Georgia who gave up her art career and her fiancé to follow God's call to Africa. She ended up in Egypt, and in a story very similar to George Muller's, began an orphanage run completely on God's provision. She spent most of her life in Egypt raising her orphans even through both world wars. At the end of her life, she had almost nothing to her name, but she had raised thousands of orphans, taken care of countless Egyptian widows, and led thousands to Christ, all by trusting in the Lord and living in surrender to him. Her's was a life well spent.

I want to point out two things from the examples of these lives. First, there is more to these amazing believers' walk with Christ than what I have been saying here. They gave up everything for Jesus and were surrendered completely to him, and they often walked by the Spirit in close intimacy with Christ. This was the foundation and spring of their lives. But there is more. Hudson Taylor found great comfort in the reality of being in Christ. This wonderful truth carried him through much of his ministry. George Muller knew the power of prayer, and this drove his life and ministry. Lillian Trasher learned to trust fully in the Lord and lean on his power rather than her own efforts. I have been fairly single minded in this piece of writing, but I want to be clear that there is more. I believe intimacy with Christ drives all other heavenly endeavors and that it is the foundation to ministry, but there are more spiritual truths and practices that flow from intimacy with Christ that I have not the time nor the knowledge to speak of here.

Second, we began all of this by saying that intimacy with Christ is the greatest gift we can give this world. It is the secret to making an eternal impact on the world. I also said that this impact is more than the usual helping someone with their groceries. People without the Holy Spirit can do that just as well as those with him. That being said, I want to point out that if we looked at the daily lives of these Spirit-filled people, we would find normal people. George Muller was a local pastor in Bristol. He spent his days visiting church members, having tea, preparing sermons, playing with kids, managing the books, and so forth.

All In

Hudson Taylor was a doctor and spent a good amount of time practicing medicine. He also spent years as an administrator when none could be found for the mission. Lillian Trasher spent most of her time looking after kids, washing clothes, and taking care of her children's many needs. Their lives probably often looked like waking up, getting ready for the day, going to work, and then going to bed.

So what made them different? Why can we look at the product of their lives and say, "Wow, God used them to change the world." In short, they knew the Lord and were daily submitted to him. Like Stephen's or Moses's faces shining, their lives shone. When God first tugged on George Muller's heart to start a Bible and breakfast club for orphans, he obeyed. When God put a vision in his heart to start an orphanage that would be funded entirely on prayer, he obeyed. He knew God and his power, and he was living a life fully submitted to him. George spent his life in the presence of God, and he was an available servant for God. He was not preoccupied building his own kingdom, his own career, or family, or security, or anything else. He was available to the Lord, and so the Lord used him. We would find this to be the same in Hudson Taylor's and Lillian Trasher's lives. In saying all of this, I hope to communicate that the world-changing impact of living a life of intimacy with the Lord may mean that most of our lives are consumed with what we call "the daily grind" of ordinary life, but throughout that daily routine

God will use us in most extraordinary ways if we live lives in close communion with him.

There are many more examples than these three, and we could go on and on. But as the writer of Hebrews says, what more should I say? For time would fail me to tell of Brother Yun, Mary, Lucius, C.T. Studd, Paul, and the countless others whose stories have either been written or faded from the memory of history, people who by the power of the Holy Spirit leapt over ten-foot prison walls, teleported while traveling for the gospel, raised the dead, raised thousands of orphans, produced cash flows equal to the largest companies on nothing but prayer, shared the gospel with the result of entire societies being transformed, people who knew God and were available for God to use. I use these three examples for us to hopefully catch a tangible glimpse of what intimacy with Christ can do. For, most of these people had very little formal training or extraordinary skills. They were ordinary people with an extraordinary God. But they did what Jesus said his followers should do: "Whoever believes in me will also do the works that I do; and greater works than these will he do" (John 14:12). Why? Because "I am going to the Father" (John 14:12). Through Jesus we have the same access to God that he did. We have access to the same Spirit. If we use our privilege to "remain in him," we will bear much fruit.

At this point let me caution you. Looking at the works of these people, we might be tempted to replicate their extraordinary lives on our own steam. If we do, we will fail. We might even try to gain intimacy with Christ through trying really hard to have a good relationship with him. This is folly. The Bible says we are in Christ. We are bound to him. He will never forsake us. If we go searching the streets with the intent of bribing him to come into our house by what good friends we would be or by how clean our house is, we will never find him. Why? Well, he is not out in the streets. He is already at our door. "Behold, I stand at the door and knock. If anyone hears my voice and opens the door, I will come in…" (Revelation 3:20). We don't need to work to get him into our house. We need only open the door. And trying hard is not the key to doing great things. A seminary education is not the key for being prepared for ministry, neither is any degree, internship, or anything else. "Now when they saw the boldness of Peter and John, and perceived that they were uneducated, common men, they were astonished. And they recognized that they had been with Jesus" (Acts 4:13). Being with Jesus is the key.

Throughout all of this I have been trying to prove only one point: being with Jesus is the real qualification for ministry; knowing Jesus will lead to world-changing transformation; intimacy with Christ is the greatest gift we can give this world. I hope by now you understand this and have some idea on how to "draw near to God" (James 4:8). But I think it is fitting to end with this point coming out of Jesus' own mouth: "I am the vine;

you are the branches. If you remain in me and I in you, you will bear much fruit; apart from me you can do nothing" (John 15:5).

Daniel Bartlett

APPENDIX

"Turn my eyes from looking at worthless things; and give me life in your ways." -Psalm 119:37

"Let no one deceive himself. If anyone among you thinks that he is wise in this age, let him become a fool that he may become wise. For the wisdom of this world is folly with God." -1 Corinthians 3:18-19

"Do not be deceived: God is not mocked, for whatever one sows, that will he also reap. For the

one who sows to his own flesh will from the flesh reap destruction, but the one who sows to the Spirit will from the Spirit reap eternal life." -Galatians 6:7-8

"Do you not know that in a race all the runners run, but only one receives the prize? So run that you may obtain it. Every athlete exercises self-control in all things. They do it to receive a perishable wreath, but we an imperishable. So I do not run aimlessly; I do not box as one beating the air. But I discipline my body and keep it under control, lest after preaching to others I myself should be disqualified." -1 Corinthians 9:24-27

All In

"But be doers of the word, and not hearers only, deceiving yourselves. For if anyone is a hearer of the word and not a doer, he is like a man who looks intently at his natural face in a mirror. For he looks at himself and goes away and at once forgets what he was like. But the one who looks intently at the perfect law, the law of liberty, and perseveres, being no hearer who forgets but a doer who acts, he will be blessed in his doing. If anyone thinks he is religious and does not bridle his tongue but deceives his heart, this person's religion is worthless. Religion that is pure and undefiled before God the Father is this: to visit orphans and widows in their affliction, and to keep oneself unstained from the world." -James 1:22-27

"'Lord, will those who are saved be few?' And He said to them, 'Strive to enter through the narrow door. For many, I tell you, will seek to enter and will not be able." -Luke 13:23-24

"Let the lowly brother boast in his exaltation, and the rich in his humiliation, because like a flower of the grass he will pass away. For the sun rises with its scorching heat and withers the grass; its flower falls and its beauty perishes. So also will the rich man fade away in the midst of his pursuits." -James 1:9-11

"But watch yourselves lest your hearts be weighed down with dissipation and drunkenness and

cares of this life, and that day come upon you suddenly like a trap." -Luke 21:34

"What good is it, my brothers, if someone says he has faith but does not have works? Can that faith save him? If a brother or sister is poorly clothed and lacking in daily food, and one of you says to them, 'Go in peace, be warmed and filled,' without giving them the things needed for the body, what good is that? So also faith by itself, if it does not have works, is dead. But someone will say, 'You have faith and I have works.' Show me your faith apart from your works, and I will show you my faith by my works. You believe that God is one; you do well. Even the demons believe—and shudder! Do you want to be shown, you foolish

person, that faith apart from works is useless? Was not Abraham our father justified by works when he offered up his son Isaac on the altar? You see that faith was active along with his works, and faith was completed by his works; and the Scripture was fulfilled that says, 'Abraham believed God, and it was counted to him as righteousness'—and he was called a friend of God. You see that a person is justified by works and not by faith alone. And in the same way was not also Rahab the prostitute justified by works when she received the messengers and sent them out by another way? For as the body apart from the spirit is dead, so also faith apart from works is dead." -James 2:14-26

"And he told this parable: 'A man had a fig tree planted in his vineyard, and he came seeking fruit on it and found none. And he said to the vinedresser, "Look, for three years now I have come seeking fruit on this fig tree, and I find none. Cut it down. Why should it use up the ground?" And he answered him, "Sir, let it alone this year also, until I dig around it and put on manure. Then if it should bear fruit next year, well and good; but if not, you can cut it down." -Luke 13:6-9

"You ask and do not receive, because you ask wrongly, to spend it on your passions. You adulterous people! Do you not know that

friendship with the world is enmity with God? Therefore whoever wishes to be a friend of the world makes himself an enemy of God." -James 4:3-4

All In

Daniel Bartlett

EndNotes

1. All Bible quotations are from the ESV except a handful which are my own translations from the Greek or Hebrew. These are noted in the text when they occur.

2. Comer, John Mark. *Live No Lies*. Waterbrook, 2021, pp. 110.

3. Writer and speaker Andy Crouch has much to say on the difference between work and rest and toil and leisure.

Daniel Bartlett

About The Author

Daniel Bartlett lives with his family in Hannibal, Missouri.

Daniel Bartlett